GW01460035

Extracting the Essence of the Śruti

The Śrutisārasamuddharaṇam of Toṭakācārya

Extracting the Essence of the Śruti

The Śrutisārasamuddharaṇam of Toṭakācārya

Translation and Commentary
by
MICHAEL COMANS

Foreword by
Swami Paramārthānanda

MOTILAL BANARSIDASS PUBLISHERS
PRIVATE LIMITED • DELHI

First Edition: Delhi, 1996

ISBN: 81-208-1410-x

Also available at:

MOTILAL BANARSIDASS
41 U.A. Bungalow Road, Jawahar Nagar, Delhi 110 007
120 Royapettah High Road, Mylapore, Madras 600 004
16 St. Mark's Road, Bangalore 560 001
8 Camac Street, Calcutta 700 017
Ashok Rajpath, Patna 800 004
Chowk, Varanasi 221 001

PRINTED IN INDIA
BY JAINENDRA PRAKASH JAIN AT SHRI JAINENDRA PRESS,
A-45 NARAINA, PHASE I, NEW DELHI 110 028
AND PUBLISHED BY NARENDRA PRAKASH JAIN FOR
MOTILAL BANARSIDASS PUBLISHERS PRIVATE LIMITED,
BUNGALOW ROAD, DELHI 110 007

THIS BOOK IS DEDICATED TO

SWAMI DAYANANDA SARASWATI

WHO BRINGS THE TRADITIONAL TEACHING

OF ADVAITA INTO THE MODERN WORLD

CONTENTS

FOREWORD

We look upon the Vedas as scriptures revealed for the benefit of humanity. The Vedas consist of two portions. The first portion is called Vedapūrva. The last portion is called Vedānta. Vedapūrva deals with a religious way of life which will contribute to the growth of society as well as the individual. Such a life will prepare a person for the philosophical enquiry dealt with in the Vedānta. This philosophical enquiry leads to the discovery of the fact that the Truth behind the microcosm and the macrocosm is one and the same. This is revealed in the form of the oneness of the individual Self *(jīvātmā)* and the universal Self *(paramātmā).* The discovery of this fact is the *summum bonum* of the Vedic way of living as it releases a person from all inner shackles. Hence Vedānta is known as Upaniṣad, the destroyer of bondage. Veda, which has come down to us in the form of oral tradition, is also called Śruti (that which is heard). Thus oneness of the individual Self and the universal Self *(jīvātma-paramātma-aikyam)* is Śrutisāra, the ultimate purport of the Vedas.

This Śrutisāra has been taken out and systematically presented to us by many teachers belonging to the beginningless preceptor-disciple lineage *(guru-śiṣya-paramparā).* The most eminent teacher in this great lineage is Ādi Śaṅkarācārya whose pioneering commentaries on the *Bhagavadgītā*, the Upaniṣads and the *Brahmasūtras* are monumental. Among the many illustrious disciples of Śaṅkarācārya, Toṭakācārya occupies a prominent position. Though not a prolific writer, he is gratefully remembered in the tradition for his pithy Vedāntic work titled *Śrutisārasamuddharaṇam.* This work, consisting of 179 verses, is in the rhythmic Toṭaka metre reminding us of the author's name.

Śrutisārasamuddharaṇam, as the title reveals, is a work which extracts the essence of the Vedic teaching viz. *jīvātma-paramātma-aikyam.* This has been done through a brilliant analysis of the famous statement *"tat tvam asi"* occurring in the *Chāndogya* Upaniṣad (6.8.7). The nature of *jīvātmā (tvam),* the nature of *paramātmā (tat)* and their essential oneness *(asi)* are brought out clearly in this work. Other possible interpretations are also considered and are ably refuted through convincing arguments. This is one of the reasons this work occupies an important place in Advaita literature.

Dr Michael Comans is known to me for the last decade or more and we have been in regular contact exchanging our views. Both of us are fortunate to be the disciples of H.H. Swami Dayananda Saraswati, a great teacher, who makes the traditional teaching available in English to the modern world without compromising with the original. Michael has published many articles on Vedānta in reputed journals and his doctoral thesis on the book *Advaitāmoda* is a valuable addition to Vedāntic literature. His commentary on the *Śrutisārasamuddharaṇam* is brief, clear and to the point. I am happy to introduce and recommend this work to the students of Vedānta.

With Nārāyaṇasmṛtis,
Swami Paramarthananda
Madras. 16.9.95

INTRODUCTION

According to Advaita tradition the *Śrutisārasamuddharaṇam* was composed by Toṭakācārya, a direct disciple of Ādi Śaṅkarācārya.[1] Toṭaka's original name was Giri. It seems that among the students of Śaṅkara, Giri was not known for his intellectual ability, but he was one who used to especially render personal service to his guru. There is no way of discovering whether such tales have any factual content, though Toṭaka does tell us: "I composed the *Śrutisārasamuddharaṇa* (Extracting the Essence of the Śruti) by listening to the discussions that took place between the teacher and students, discussions that were like *śruti* itself" (v.175). Perhaps from this we can surmise that he used to listen to the learned discussions but not take much part in them himself. At the end of the *Śrutisārasamuddharaṇam* he speaks about the necessity of devotion to the guru, so perhaps the legendary account of his personality was built up from these sources.

The story goes that Śaṅkara was one day sitting with his students, ready to commence a class explaining his commentary upon the *Brahmasūtra*. They all sat for some time but Śaṅkara did not start the class. Padmapāda, one of the most eminent students of Śaṅkara, indicated to Śaṅkara that the time for the class to commence had passed. Śaṅkara said, "Let us wait for Giri to come." Giri was still at the river bank washing the master's clothes. Padmapāda motioned towards the wall and replied, "Let the wall stand in for Giri." Śaṅkara understood Padmapāda's sarcasm but said nothing and they continued to wait. Śaṅkara thought he would teach Padmapāda a lesson and by means of some extraordinary power he inspired the mind of Giri as he was returning from the river with the clothes. When Giri appeared he was spontaneously composing verse after verse in praise of his guru. Padmapāda was no doubt astonished and felt suitably chastened. These verses, known as the *Toṭakāṣṭakam*, were composed in a difficult but melodious metre known as Toṭaka and Giri was thereafter called Toṭaka. Shortly after this event, he composed the *Śrutisārasamuddharaṇam*, consisting of one hundred and seventy-nine verses, all in the Toṭaka metre except for the first verse (in *Vasantatilakā)* and the last two verses (in *Sragdharā).*

The *Śrutisārasamuddharaṇam* (which we shall for convenience hereafter abbreviate to *"Śrutisāra")* is in the form of a dialogue between a Vedānta guru and a *sannyāsī* who has come to him as a seeker. The prose portion of Śaṅkara's *Upadeśasāhasrī* is also composed as a dialogue and it would seem that these compositions, recreating as they do discussions between the guru and the student, tell us something about the way of teaching at that time. Apart from the rather formal and standard opening of the *Śrutisāra* where the student approaches the guru and requests instruction in the conventional manner, and the closing verses where the student expresses his delight to the teacher, the rest of the work manages for the most part to create the feeling of an interaction between the guru and the student. As the text progresses, the student raises questions, objections, and, very occasionally, interrupts the guru to put a further question. The text is skilfully arranged, flowing from topic to topic and engaging the reader as the witness to an, at times, animated discussion.

The *Śrutisāra* has three principal topics and various subsidiary topics. The principal topics are: (1) the discovery of the Self as the invariable Witness *(sākṣī)* of the mind and its activities (vv. 5-47); (2) the determination of the correct meaning of the sentence *"tat tvam asi"* (vv.48-106); (3) the understanding that the Self is identical to what is meant by the word Brahman (vv.107-113), and the ascertainment of the *mithyātva* of the world by means of following the reasoning implicit in the *śruti* (vv.117-132) as well as by independent reasoning (vv.133-157). Following the discussion about the *mithyātva* of the world, Toṭaka again takes up the topic of the identity of the meanings of *tat* and *tvam* (vv.158-159) and he talks of *jīvanmukti* and the understanding of the *jīvanmukta* (vv.160-167). He then sums up (vv.168-171) and the student expresses his gratitude at receiving and understanding the teaching (vv.172-174).

In the section discussing the meaning of *"tat tvam asi"*, the guru refutes various alternative ways of understanding the sentence proposed by the student. The most important of these is that the sentence does not speak about reality and reveal "you are Brahman", but the sentence is only a type of metaphor enjoining some sort of conceptual meditation *(upāsana).* Toṭaka refutes this contention at length. The fact that he devotes so many verses to this matter is an indication of the age of the work. It is well known that the refutation of certain views of the Pūrva Mīmāṁsakas figures prominently in the commentaries of Śaṅkara (for example, his commentary on *Brahmasūtra* 1.1.4). Śaṅkara is particularly concerned to combat the Mīmāṁsaka doctrine that the entire Veda is just concerned with the performance of the Vedic rites and consequently the statements found in the Upaniṣads that reveal the nature of Brahman and the identity of the Self with Brahman have to be interpreted only within the context of the performance of the Vedic ritual. According to the Pūrva Mīmāṁsakas, statements such as *"tat tvam asi"* do not actually deal with metaphysical reality but are just meant as conceptual meditations to be performed by the sacrificer in the course of the ritual. Toṭaka, like Śaṅkara, gives considerable attention to the refutation of such a position and in doing so he indicates that the *Śrutisāra* is a work belonging to the same period as Śaṅkara, when the refutation of such doctrines of the Pūrva Mīmāṁsā was a primary concern for the follower of the Upaniṣads.[2]

In regard to the *Śrutisāra,* there is one point in particular that ought be mentioned. As one of the principal arguments for demonstrating the *mithyātva* of the world Toṭaka argues, on the basis of the *śruti,* that the material cause is real and its products are unreal *(mithyā).* Toṭaka says that Brahman is real because Brahman is the material cause of the world and the world is unreal because it is a product (v.126). We know that a material cause, like gold etc., undergoes transformation into the form of its effects. Does that mean that Brahman too undergoes transformation in relation to the world? If Brahman undergoes transformation then Brahman would not be changeless, and without being changeless Brahman could not be permanent (i.e. eternal). European scholars have noted that Śaṅkara does not use the term *"vivarta"* which became the standard term in later Advaita to refer to an apparent transformation, when something appears to transform into something else while all the while not relinquishing its original condition *(svasvarūpāparityāgena rūpāntarāpattiḥ),* like how the rope seems to become the snake. But even though Śaṅkara does not use the word *vivarta,* there can be no doubt that he maintains that Brahman undergoes no transformation (cf., for example,

Brahmasūtrabhāṣya 2.1.14 and 2.1.27).[3] So too Toṭaka says on five separate occasions that the Self [identical in nature to Brahman] is untransformed (vv.7, 8, 10, 34, 47) and by his juxtaposition of the words "material cause" and "permanent" *(dhruva)* we should understand that Brahman is the unchanged material cause. So even though they did not use the word *"vivarta"* they can only have taught that the world is an apparent transformation of Brahman.

As far as I know, the *Śrutisāra* has been translated twice before, the first translation is a very free rendering and the other translation is hardly available.[4] In this translation I have tried to retain some of the flavour of the original, though we must not forget that the translation is of necessity in prose, whereas Toṭaka managed to convey all this teaching through verse! A feature of this work is the commentary in English explaining the text verse by verse. This commentary is not intended to satisfy academicians but it is written to assist people who may wish to understand the text in the absence of a competent authority to explain it to them. My hope is that it will go some way in achieving this purpose.

In reading the *Śrutisāra* I obtained much help from the Sanskrit commentary of Saccidānandayogīndra. Nothing is known about the commentator. The colophon of the Ānandāśrama edition tells us that he was a student of Śrī Pūrṇātmayogīndra,[5] so it would seem that he belongs to the *indrasarasvatī* line of *sannyāsins* from Kaṇci. His commentary is particularly lucid and although it contains a couple of errors, as pointed out in the English introduction to the Vani Vilas Edition (Sri Rangam), it is a fine commentary that deserves to be reprinted, with those errors noted, in future Sanskrit editions of the *Śrutisārasamuddharaṇam.* I also found help in the Kailās Āśram edition of the text with the Hindi commentary of Swami Vidyānandagiri. I would like to thank Archana Parashar for assisting my poor Hindi by reading much of this commentary with me. I would also like to thank my esteemed friend and *gurubhai,* Swami Paramārthānanda, of Madras, for gracing this book with a Foreword and for clarifying some points for me here and there along the way.

Technical Notes

Most of the *Śrutisārasamuddharaṇam* is in the form of a conversation, analogous to the form of direct speech in a text such as the *Bhagavad Gītā.* Verses 4 through to 170 are in direct speech and 171 through 174 are mostly in direct speech. Quotation marks have not been used to indicate direct speech.

The text of the *Śrutisārasamuddharaṇam* as given here follows the edition of the Sri Vani Vilas Press except where the reading of the Ānandāśrama edition was thought preferable. At one place the reading from the Kailās Āśram edition was adopted in preference to the other two editions. On a couple of occasions, a copy of the manuscript of the *Śrutisārasamuddharaṇam* from the Bhandarkar Research Institute [No.127 of 1902.1907] was also consulted. The text as printed here does not constitute a new critical edition, as it is essentially based upon the Vani Vilas and the Ānandāśram printed texts. A list of the variant readings between these two editions is provided in the Appendix.

---

1 J Bader mentions that of the eight major legendary accounts of the life of Śaṅkarācārya, all except Anantānandagiri's *Śaṅkaravijaya* mention Toṭaka as a direct disciple of Śaṅkara. Jonathan Bader, *Conquest of the Four Quarters: Traditional Accounts of the Life of Śaṅkara,* unpublished Ph.D. thesis, Australian National University, 1991, p.52. Advaita literature accepts Toṭaka as a disciple of Ādi Śaṅkara eg. *Advaita Grantha Kośa,* Kanci, (n.d.) p.140. R. Thangaswami, *A Bibliographical Survey of Advaita Vedanta Literature,* Madras: Univ. of Madras, 1980, p.232. T.M.P. Mahadevan (ed.) *Preceptors of Advaita,* Secunderabad: Sri Kanci Kamakoti Shankara Mandir, 1968, p.63ff.

2 I would like to express an opinion concerning a work which is popularly, but most probably erroneously, considered to be a work of Ādi Śaṅkara. The work I am referring to is the *Vivekacūḍāmaṇi.* There are a number of reasons why this is not a

genuine work of Ādi Śaṅkara. In ascending order of importance these are as follows. (a) The style of the verses of the *Vivekacūḍāmaṇi* is highly poetic in contrast to the vigorous but not especially graceful style of the verses in the *Upadeśasāhasrī*, a work universally accepted as the composition of Ādi Śaṅkara. Someone may argue that Śaṅkara's style could have changed and point out that Śaṅkara's hymns are very poetic compositions. However this does not constitute sufficient proof, since the hymns themselves are not universally accepted as the compositions of Ādi Śaṅkara. (b) The fact that there are very few commentaries on the *Vivekacūḍāmaṇi*, and no old commentaries by well known Advaita authors, would tend to indicate that the *Vivekacūḍāmaṇi* is not the composition of Ādi Śaṅkara and is in fact not a very old work. (c) Some aspects of the teaching of the *Vivekacūḍāmaṇi* are foreign to other works of Śaṅkara or are contradictory to them. The series of verses in the *Vivekacūḍāmaṇi* extolling the importance of yogic-type *nirvikalpa samādhi* (eg. vv.341-42, 353-57, 360-63) sit at variance with the minimal importance Śaṅkara gives to *samādhi* practices in his other works. The statements belittling the importance of hearing the Upaniṣads (cf. v.364) would contradict his teachings in his commentary upon *Brahmasūtra* 4.1.2 and the whole theme of the lengthy eighteenth chapter of the *Upadeśasāhasrī*. Thus the *Vivekacūḍāmaṇi*, for all its undoubted merit as a manual explaining Vedānta, is not likely to be a composition of Ādi Śaṅkara and is more than likely to be a composition of some later Śaṅkarācārya, perhaps connected to the Śriṅgeri *pīṭham*. One of the Śriṅgeri Śaṅkarācāryas, Abhinava Nṛsiṁha Bhāratī 1 (who adorned the *pīṭham* from 1599-1622) founded a branch *maṭha* in Śivagaṅga and placed his disciple Śaṅkara Bhāratī, who took *sannyāsa* in 1615 and was himself an eminent scholar, in charge of this *maṭha* (cf. K.R. Venkataraman, *The Throne of Transcendental Wisdom: Śrī Śaṁkarācārya's Śāradā Pīṭha in Śriṅgeri*, Sringeri: Sri Sharada Trust , 3rd Ed., 1990, p.77). The concluding verse of the *Vivekacūḍāmaṇi* (v.580) contains the phrase *"eṣā śaṅkarabhāratī vijayate"* which is generally understood to mean that the "voice of Śaṅkara is victorious", referring to the teaching of Śaṅkara. However the word *"śaṅkarabhāratī"* could be a *double entendre (śleṣa)* referring also to the name of the author. This is a matter for research scholars to determine.

3 J.L. Shastri (ed.), *Brahmasūtra-Śāṅkarabhāṣyam*, Delhi: Motilal Banarsidass, 1980. 2.1.14, p.380, line 5ff.; 2.1.27, p.401, line 7ff. Also, note his contrast between *pariṇāminityam* and *kūṭasthanityam* in 1.1.4, p.72f., line 7ff.

4 The first translation is by Swami Brahmānanda, *Revelation of the Ever Revealed,* Rishikesh: Divine Life Society, 1978. The second is by Kumari R. Pattammal, "Sri Totakacarya's Srutisarasamuddharanam", serialised in *The Voice of Śaṅkara (Śaṅkara-bhāratī):* A Quarterly Journal of Advaita-Vedānta, Vol. V11, Nos.1-4, 1983 and Vol.V111, 1984. I have only seen a small portion of this work, for it is not easy to come by, but it appears to be an accurate translation with notes.

5 The colophon of the Vani Vilas edition says that he was a student of Śrī Pūjyapādayogīndra.

DETAILED TABLE OF CONTENTS

12-13 Argument against Buddhists to show that Awareness and cognition are distinct.

14-15. The nature of the mind: it has two types of cognition, *idaṁvṛtti* and *ahaṁvṛtti.*

16-20. The ego-notion *(ahaṁvṛtti)* is natural to transactional life.

21. Is the ego-notion an attribute of Awareness, or is it an attribute of the mind?

22-24. The reason why the ego-notion cannot be an attribute of Awareness.

25-26. The doctrine of the Vaiśeṣika, that the Self possesses various attributes, is not tenable.

27-30. Refutation of the proposition that the Self has attributes due to the existence of a relation called conjunction *(saṁyoga)* between the Self and the mind.

31. The *siddhānta* of those who know the *śruti* is that Brahman alone is real and 'everything else' is unreal.

32. The Vaiśeṣika doctrine is rejected.

33. Restatement of the reason why the ego-notion cannot be an attribute of the Self.

34. The established position of the Advaita.

35. Question by the student as to how the embodied self can be said to be identical to Brahman. The teacher replies.

60. The student objects that the grammatical apposition between *tat* and *tvam* in the sentence *"tat tvam asi"* would indicate that the *jīva* is unreal.

61-67. The teacher replies that the grammatical apposition between two terms expresses the unreality of one of the terms only if there is the relationship of material cause and its effect between the two terms. But this is not the case in the sentence *"tat tvam asi"*.

68. The student asks what then do the *mahavākyas* like *"tat tvam asi"* communicate if there is no difference at all between the individual Self and Brahman?

69-72. The teacher replies that a if there is a real difference between the *jīva* and Brahman, words would not be able to remove that difference. What the *mahāvākya* does is negate falsely superimposed difference.

73. The teacher says that *"tat tvam asi"* is not meant as an *upāsana*, nor is it a metaphor, nor a type of praise.

74-81. The teacher answers the objection (put forward in verse 52) and refutes the idea that *"tat tvam asi"* could be saying that Brahman is really a *jīva*.

82-85. The teacher answers the objection raised in verse 53.

86-90. The teacher again takes up the topic that *tat tvam asi* is not meant to be an *upāsana*, because the sentence *"tat tvam asi"* contains no injunction to do something.

91-94. The teacher says that even though there is no injunction it should not be thought that the sentence has no benefit. The benefit is the removal of *saṁsāra*.

115. The three states are unreal because they are attributes of the unreal mind.

116-124. Explanation of the *Chāndogya* Upaniṣad (6.4.1-3) passage which teaches that the material cause is real and its products are *mithyā.*

125. The example of threads and cloth show that the product is unreal.

126-127. Summary of the topic that the *śruti* teaches that the material cause is real while its products are *mithyā.*

128. Since the mind is unreal, its product, the three states, must therefore be unreal.

129. The student objects that the mind is not unreal because the *śruti* does not say that the mind is a product.

130-132. The teacher replies that the *śruti* does teach that the mind is a product.

133-134. The teacher presents an inference to demonstrate that the world is *mithyā* because a product does not exist separate from its material cause.

135-136. Argument directed against the followers of Nyāya who hold that the product is something additional to the material cause.

137. The student objects that a product is different from its material cause since the product has a name, a form and a function distinct from its material cause.

138-140. The teacher shows that the product is not something other than its material cause.

Śrutisārasamuddharaṇam

त्रैलोक्यनाथहरिमीड्यमुदारसत्त्वं
शक्तेस्तनूजतनयं परमेष्ठिकल्पम् ।
जीमूतमुक्तविमलाम्बरचारुवर्णं
वासिष्ठमुग्रतपसं प्रणतोऽस्मि नित्यम् ॥१॥

I bow down always to Hari, the Lord of the three worlds, who is worthy of praise and whose qualities are most exalted. I always bow to the grandson of Śakti, who is himself alike to the supreme Lord, whose complexion is delightful like the pure sky free from clouds, who belongs to the lineage of Vasiṣṭha and who has undergone the most intense austerity. (1)

comment

It is customary for an author to commence his work with an introductory verse, known as *maṅgalācaraṇa,* in which the author salutes his special deity and his teacher. Here, Toṭaka pays homage to Viṣṇu and to the sage Vyāsa. This verse indicates the lineage of the Vedānta tradition, which is said to commence with Viṣṇu-Nārāyaṇa Himself and has been passed down through a succession of teachers. There was a father-son relation among some of these early teachers, for it is said that Śakti was the eldest of the sons of the sage Vasiṣṭha and that Śakti in turn had a son, Parāśara, who is traditionally believed to have composed the *Viṣṇupurāṇa* and the *Parāśarasmṛti.* Vyāsa was the son of Parāśara. Vyāsa is also known as Kṛṣṇadvaipāyana because he was said to be dark in colour *(kṛṣṇa)* and born on an island *(dvaipāyana).* He is also known as Vedavyāsa since he is said to have arranged the Veda into four groups:

Rg, Yajus, Sāma and *Atharva.* He is also believed to have composed the *Brahmasūtra*, the *Mahābhārata* and most of the major *Purāṇas.* He had a son, Śuka who, because of his great detachment, did not marry or produce children.

In the Advaita tradition *(sampradāya)* there is a well known verse which gives the lineage of teachers *(guruparaṁparā).* This verse is recited even in present times at the commencement of the study of certain texts:

> I continually bow down to Nārāyaṇa, to the one who was born from a lotus [Brahmā], to Vasiṣṭha, to Śakti and to his son Parāśara, to Vyāsa, to Śuka, to the great Gauḍapāda, to Govinda the best of yogis, then to his student Śrī Śaṅkarācārya, then to his students Padmapāda and Hastāmalaka, Toṭaka and the Vārttikakāra [Sureśvara] and others [up to and including] my own teacher.

Toṭaka now begins the text.

सकलं मनसा क्रियया जनितं समवेक्ष्य विनाशितया तु जगत् ।
निरविद्यत कश्चिदतो निखिलादविनाशि कृतेन न लभ्यमिति ॥२॥

Someone, upon discerning that the entire world produced by action is perishable, became dispassionate towards everything [knowing that] nothing imperishable can be obtained by action. (2)

comment

This verse is closely modelled upon the first half of a passage from the *Muṇḍaka* Upaniṣad which says:

> A Brāhmaṇa, upon examining the worlds won through actions, would become dispassionate [thinking that] there is nothing uncreated (i.e. eternal) through action. (1.2. 12)

Toṭaka's verse presents the attitude of the mature student who sees that whatever can be gained by action is invariably limited. Whatever can be gained by an action is limited in three ways. It is limited to the place where it occurs *(deśa)*, it is limited to a duration of time *(kāla)* and it is limited by the inherently finite nature of the result itself *(vastu).* Any accomplishment is thus intrinsically finite. The statement that the world is "produced by action" means that our present circumstances are the result of our actions *(karmaphala)* performed at some previous time. Not only are the circumstances of this life transient, but according to the Upaniṣads even heaven is not a permanent abode. Heaven is won through virtuous actions, but since the results of all actions are limited by time, even the reward of heaven will be impermanent. There is a frequently quoted passage in the *Chāndogya* Upaniṣad which says:

> Just as here, the world won by action perishes, so too there, the world won by virtuous deeds perishes. (8.1.6)

The *Bhagavadgītā* also says:

> When the result of their virtuous deeds is exhausted, they enter the mortal world. (9.21)

Toṭaka, following the *Muṇḍaka* passage, says that some rare person, perceiving that everything produced by action is impermanent, becomes dispassionate towards all the goals which the world holds dear and the means to acquire them. The reason for this dispassion is given in the last line of the verse: "nothing imperishable can be obtained by action."

What does such a person do?

प्रतिपित्सुरसावविनाशि पदं यतिधर्मरतो यतिमेव गुरुम् ।
विदितात्मसतत्त्वमुपेत्य कविं प्रणिपत्य निवेदितवान्स्वमतम् ॥३॥

Desiring to know That which is imperishable, he took to the discipline of the renunciate's way of life and approached a teacher who was himself a renunciate, who knew the true nature of the Self and who had both learning and insight. Having prostrated to the teacher he informed him about what he was thinking. (3)

comment

This verse follows the second half of the *Muṇḍaka* passage, which says:

> In order to clearly know the eternal he should, taking sacrificial fuel in his hand, approach a teacher who is learned in the scriptures and established in Brahman. (1. 2. 12)

Toṭaka indicates that the seeker has taken, or at least wishes to take to the life of renunciation *(sannyāsa).* Śaṅkara, in the prose part of his work the *Upadeśasāhasrī,* mentions the adoption of a renunciate's life as one of the qualifications required to pursue the knowledge of Brahman, though in the same work he also speaks of a celibate student *(brahmacārī)* approaching a teacher to gain this knowledge. There is obviously some flexibility in the matter. This is borne out in the Upaniṣads themselves where there are instances of householders approaching sages in order to know Brahman, such as in the *Muṇḍaka* Upaniṣad (1.1.3) where the sage Aṅgiras taught the wealthy householder Śaunaka.

Toṭaka indicates that here the spiritual teacher *(guru)* is also a renunciate and is a person who "knows the true nature of the Self and who has both learning and insight". The *Muṇḍaka* Upaniṣad specifies that the seeker should go to a *guru* who possesses two important qualifications: the *guru* should be "learned in the scriptures *(śrotriya)* and established in Brahman *(brahmaniṣṭha)".* In the prose part of the *Upadeśasāhasrī,* Śaṅkara elaborates upon the qualifications required of a spiritual teacher:

> The teacher is one who can see an issue from both sides, who can grasp what is said and is retentive. He is tranquil, self-controlled, compassionate and helpful etc. He is one who has received the traditional teaching. He is not attached to enjoyments whether in this world or in another world and he has renounced all rites and the means by which rites are performed. He is a knower of Brahman and is established in Brahman. His conduct is not other than what it seems, he is completely free from such defects as pretension, pride, deceit, cruelty, trickery, jealousy, false speech, egoity and attachment etc. As his sole purpose is to help others, he wishes to make available the knowledge [of Brahman].

He addresses the teacher.

भगवन्नुदधौ मृतिजन्मजले सुखदुःखझषे पतितं व्यथितम् ।
कृपया शरणागतमुद्धर मामनुशाध्युपसन्नमनन्यगतिम् ॥४॥

Holy one, I have fallen into an ocean whose waters are birth and death and where the fish are pleasures and pains. I am sorely distressed. Please help me, I have come for refuge! You must teach me as I have come to you and there is no one else to whom I can turn! (4)

The teacher commences his instruction.

विनिवर्त्य रतिं विषये विषमां परिमुच्य शरीरनिबद्धमतिम् ।
परमात्मपदे भव नित्यरतो जहि मोहमयं भ्रममात्ममतेः ॥५॥

Having put a stop to the painful attraction to sense-objects and having given up identifying yourself with the body, always find delight in the Supreme Self. You must abandon the error, the product of delusion, through knowledge of the Self. (5)

comment

The teacher puts the teaching in a nutshell. He says that the student should cease his attraction towards sense-objects and give up identifying himself with the body. Why? Because the attraction to sense-objects and the identification with the body prevent the student from understanding his real nature and, even when the knowledge is present, they obstruct the full flowering of that understanding. The attraction to sense-objects is a type of superimposition *(adhyāsa)* known as *śobhanādhyāsa.* Superimposition is when something [A] appears in something else [B] though the former does not actually exist in the latter *(atadrūpe tadrūpāvabhāsa).* A sense-object is not intrinsically attractive because everybody does not find the same object equally attractive. What is most attractive to one person may not be attractive to someone else. This shows that a person superimposes his or her subjective ideas of what is attractive and unattractive upon the things of the world. The teacher is telling the student to stop projecting his likes and dislikes onto sense-objects.

The teacher then tells the student to give up "identifying yourself with the body". Here he is referring to the superimposition of the Self and the body where the person superimposes the body-sense-mind complex onto the Self so that there is the non metaphorical identification "I am fat", "I am thin" "I am dark", "I am fair", even though these are attributes only of the body. So too, a person superimposes the attributes of the senses, "I am deaf", "I am one-eyed", "I am blind" etc. A person also superimposes the attributes of the mind such as desire, intention, doubt, determination etc. All of the above are objects of the Self, but the person confuses them as the Self and suffers the consequences of that identification in feelings such as inadequacy, since no body-sense-mind complex is, or remains, as one would wish. In speaking of giving up identification with the body etc. the teacher is not referring to the natural identification with the body-sense-mind complex, without which a person could not carry out even everyday activities *(vyavahāra)* like walking, talking and so forth, but he is telling him to give up the superimposition that the body etc. and their attributes are the intrinsic properties of the I, the subject who objectifies them. The teacher tells the student that once he is no longer given over to hankering after sense enjoyments and is not identifying the Self with the body and its properties then he should find his delight solely in the Self.

The teacher then tells him how he can give up this superimposition. He says, "abandon the error, the product of delusion, through knowledge of the Self." The error *(bhrama)* is the above mentioned superimposition *(adhyāsa).* The "product of delusion" *(mohamaya)* means the product of ignorance *(avidyā),* the affix *maya (mayaṭ)* being used in the sense of a product *(vikāra),* as in the following verse. This superimposition, the effect of ignorance, is to be abandoned by "knowledge of the Self" for only knowledge can be the antidote for ignorance. The teacher tells the student: give up this superimposition by knowing the Self and remain thereafter enjoying your real nature.

The teacher elaborates upon what was said.

विसृजान्नमयादिषु पञ्चसु तामहमस्मि ममेति मतिं सततम् ।
दृशिरूपमनन्तमृतं विगुणं हृदयस्थमवेहि सदाहमिति ॥६॥

Constantly give up the notion of "I" and "mine" in regard to the five [sheaths] beginning with the one which is a product of food. You must have the understanding: "I am always pure Seeing, limitless, real, free from attributes, present within the heart [i.e. within the intellect]." (6)

comment

The "five beginning with food" refer to the five "sheaths" spoken of in the *Taittirīya* Upaniṣad (2.1.1-2.5.1). They are called "sheaths" or "coverings" *(kośa)* because they seem to cover the Self in so far as they are five increasingly subtle locations where we mistake the Self as the body-sense-mind complex. These five are (1) the physical body *(annamayakośa)* which is a product of part of the food that we consume. (2) The life-force within the body *(prāṇamayakośa).* The *prāṇa* performs five different functions: respiration, digestion, circulation, evacuation of waste-matter from the body, and expulsion of materials by way of vomiting etc. (3) The mind *(manomayakośa)* consists of different types of thinking such as desire, intention, doubt and determination. (4) The intellect *(vijñānamayakośa)* is distinguished from mind in so far as the intellect is said to be the type of cognition that is present when we come to know something and when we are capable of subtle thinking. The sense of doership is located in this *kośa.* (5) The fifth covering is made up of enjoyment *(ānandamayakośa)* for that too is not the Self but it is made up of the happy feelings that arise due to various circumstances. The sense of enjoyership thus belongs to this *kośa.* When we say: "I am fat", "I am thin", "I am dark", "I am fair", we identify the body and its properties with the Self. When we say: "I am hungry", "I am thirsty", "I am tired", we identify the various functions of the *prāṇa* with the Self. We identify the mind with the Self when we assume that various mental states such as willing, desiring, doubting etc. are the properties of the Self. Similarly, we identify the intellect with the Self when we assume the cognitive activity involved in knowing to be the property of the Self. We identify the feelings of enjoyment with the Self when we assume that the happy states of mind that arise in varying intensity such as like *(priya)*, gladness *(moda)* and delight *(pramoda)* are the properties of the Self. These five "coverings" present a method of analysis to help us see in which way we limit the Self by an identification based upon some condition pertaining to the body-mind.

If the absolute Self is not the body-sense-mind complex, then what is the real nature of the Self? The teacher says that the Self is: "pure Seeing", meaning pure Awareness; intrinsically "limitless" i.e. unconditioned; "real" i.e. invariable; "free from attributes" i.e. cannot be characterised as having objective properties of 'such and such' that would distinguish it from something else and thereby limit it; "present within the heart" i.e. within the intellect, for Self-knowledge, like any knowledge, takes place in the intellect.

If the Self is intrinsically of the nature of unlimited Awareness, or Brahman, then there is only one Self. But our experience is that there is a different Self in each physical body. Using two illustrations, the teacher accounts for the appearance of a multiplicity of Selves.

जलभेदकृता बहुतेव रवेर्घटिकादिकृता नभसोऽपि यथा ।
मतिभेदकृता तु तथा बहुता तव बुद्धिदृशोऽविकृतस्य सदा ॥७॥

Just as the sun seems to be manifold owing to the different [bodies of] water [where it is reflected] and just as space seems to be manifold due to the pots and so forth [which seem to divide space], so too, You, the Witness of the mind, who are always without change, seem to be manifold on account of the diversity of minds. (7)

comment

The one sun, reflecting in different pools of water, seems to be many. The undivided space seems to be divided by the forms that exist within it. Analogous to these illustrations, Brahman, pure Awareness, is not multiple. Awareness seems to be multiple because it is "reflected" *(pratibimbita)* in the subtle material of the internal-organ *(antaḥkaraṇa* - which we will hereafter just refer to as "mind") like the sun seems to be many when it is reflected in different pools of water. Or we can say that

Awareness, when "conditioned" *(avacchinna)* by the different minds, appears to be multiple, like space seems to be multiple when conditioned by the different material forms of walls etc., even though those forms do not actually delimit space.

The key term which Advaita employs to explain difference is *upādhi*, or "limiting adjunct". An *upādhi* refers to some thing [A] which apparently conditions something else [B] by transferring its own properties to that other thing due to the proximity between them. The standard illustration is of a red flower which transfers its property of redness to a clear crystal on account of their proximity. The red flower is the *upādhi* of the crystal. Thus an *upādhi* is something which seemingly conditions something else. It "seemingly conditions" because the crystal does not actually become red, it only seems to be red.

The mind is the principal *upādhi*, for in the mind the pure Awareness seems to be conditioned and thereby seems to become the individual self *(jīva)*. Brahman is thus apparently conditioned by the various *upādhis* in which it "manifests". Brahman, in association with the *upādhis* of divinities, becomes Viṣṇu, Śiva etc. The same Brahman, as associated with the *upādhis* of men and women, becomes human beings, and the same Brahman in association with the *upādhi* of animals becomes other living forms. It is the same source of life, the same unchanging Awareness, that is everywhere present. All difference is due only to the differences among the limiting adjuncts. All difference is thus *upādhibheda*, it not intrinsic.

The teacher says that You, the unchanging Witness, are always free from bondage.

दिनकृत्प्रभया सदृशेन सदा जनचित्तरतं सकलं स्वचिता ।
विदितं भविताविकृतेन सदा यत एवमतोऽसित एव सदा ॥८॥

Since You, the Awareness, who are always without change, invariably reveal the entire operations of the minds of living beings, analogous to how the light of the sun [constantly reveals its objects], You are therefore always without bondage. (8)

comment

The word "You" in the verse does not mean the "person" who looks upon himself or herself as the limited body-sense-mind complex, but the word refers to one's essential nature. The teacher says that just like the light of the sun reveals all things simultaneously, the light of Awareness reveals the minds of all beings from the deities to an insect. In this way, Awareness is spoken of as the "witness" *(sākṣī)* of the mind. The Witness-Self is unchanging and so it is "unaffected" *(aspṛṣṭa)* by whatever it reveals, like how a light reveals its object without being affected by the object. Since the Witness-Self is intrinsically unaffected, the Self is innately free from bondage, because bondage consists, in the final analysis, of the identification with the contents of the mind and the self-judgement arising from that identification.

The teacher says that Awareness is without change. Any change is something known, for if a thing changes, but that change could not be known, then we could never prove that the thing has changed. So change must be known. If Awareness changes, how is that change known? It can only be known by a second Awareness which has not changed in so far as it is able to reveal the change in the first Awareness. If we say that the second Awareness changes, then in order for that change to be revealed we will either have to postulate an infinite regress in which each Awareness is revealed by another Awareness, or we will have to say that Awareness has parts whereby one part which is unchanging reveals the other part which changes. But even then we still have to explain whether the unchanging part changes or does not change. If we say that the absence of change is just momentary and that there is actually a series of Awareness states, whereby the prior member of the series is revealed by the next member as it arises, and its cessation is in turn revealed by the next member as it arises, then we have the teaching of Buddhism that Awareness is a series of inter-dependent, momentary, states. But then we will have to account for the experience of the unity of Awareness. Advaita says that the Buddhists have failed to discriminate between cognitions and Awareness. Change belongs to the mental modes *(vṛtti)* or "thoughts" and all changes are revealed by the essential Awareness which is free from change. The teacher will go into this in some detail in the following verses.

The teacher now proceeds to explain the distinction between mind and pure Awareness. He firstly discusses the changing nature of the mind.

उपरागमपेक्ष्य मतिर्विषयैर्विषयावधृतिं कुरुते तु यतः ।
तत एव मतेर्विदिताविदिता विषयास्तु ततः परिणामवती ॥९॥

In order for the mind to ascertain the sense-objects it requires to be influenced by the sense-objects. That is why sense-objects are either known or unknown to the mind. So it is the mind that undergoes transformation. (9)

comment

How does an object become perceptually known? According to our commonsense understanding, a sense-object is external to the mind. In order to know some sense-object a relation must first be established between the appropriate sense-organ and the object. Once that relation is established, a cognition *(vṛtti)* arises in the mind and, by means of the sense-organ, the cognition envelopes the object and takes on the form of the object. So when we know a sense-object we always know it via a cognition that takes the form of the object. The cognition "taking on the form of the object" is called *viṣayākāravṛtti*, i.e. a cognition *(vṛtti)* which takes the form *(ākāra)* of the sense-object *(viṣaya)*. Objects are known only when the above conditions occur, otherwise an object remains unknown. The word *uparāga* in the verse means that in order for an object to become known the mind has to receive the impression or influence of the sense-object via the cognition. The process of perception means that the mind undergoes cognitive change. So the teacher is saying that it is the mind that changes.

The teacher says that Awareness does not undergo change.

मतिवृत्तय आत्मचिता विदिताः सततं हि यतोऽविकृतस्तु ततः ।

यदि चात्मचितिः परिणामवती मतयो विदिताविदिताः स्युरिमाः ॥१०॥

Since the cognitions of the mind are constantly revealed by the Awareness that is the Self, therefore the Self is changeless. If Awareness undergoes change, cognitions would [sometimes] be revealed and [sometimes] not be revealed. (10)

comment

The mind is made up of changing cognitions or "thoughts". They have a "form" because cognitions are always about something. It is a fact of experience that cognitions come and go. But a cognition cannot reveal its own absence. So the absence of a cognition must be revealed by something other than that cognition. According to Advaita, the Awareness, which is the essential Self, reveals both the presence and the absence of all mental forms. There is thus a "relation" of revealer and revealed between Awareness and cognitions. Does the Awareness change like the cognitions? The teacher argues that if Awareness changes, then cognitions could occur even without being revealed. But how could it be proved that such unknown cognitions occur? In accord with our experience, we say that the contents of the mind, whether in waking or in dream, are invariably revealed by Awareness.

चरितं तु धियः सकलं सततं विदितं भवता परिशुद्धचिता ।
मतिभेदगुणो न हि तेऽस्ति ततो यत एवमतोऽसदृशस्तु धिया ॥११॥

The entire operation of the mind is constantly revealed by You, the Awareness that is completely pure. Therefore the attribute belonging to the different cognitions does not belong to You. Therefore You are not the same as the mind. (11)

comment

The mind consists of thought-forms which undergo change. The changing thoughts are revealed by the constant Awareness. Awareness is said to be "completely pure" as it is inherently "untouched" or unaffected by whatever it reveals. Just as light illumines objects without being tainted by what it illumines, so too Awareness reveals the entire contents of the mind while remaining untainted by what it illumines. Since the Awareness is constant while the thoughts come and go, Awareness does not have the "the attribute belonging to the different cognitions", meaning that it does not have the attribute of change *(pariṇāma)* like thoughts have the attribute of change. Therefore Awareness and the mind are dissimilar.

The Buddhists do not accept the existence of an unchanging Awareness. They say that Awareness is not something other than the cognitions. The teacher addresses this issue in the following two verses.

विदितत्वमविप्रतिपन्नतया मतिषु प्रगतं विषयेषु यथा ।
यत एवमतः परसंविदिता विदितत्वत एव यथा विषयाः ॥१२॥

Just as there is no disagreement that sense-objects are known, it is certainly not a matter for disagreement that cognitions are known. Since this is so, it follows that the cognitions must be known by something other. The reason is the fact that they are known, just like sense-objects are known. (12)

comment

The Buddhists argue that there is no need to assume the existence of an Awareness apart from the operations of the mind itself. The cognition is itself the revealer *(grāhaka)* and the revealed *(grāhya)*, it reveals itself and its content, so it is both the subject and the object. Śaṅkara has debated this matter in various works (for example, his commentary upon *Bṛhadāraṇyaka* Upaniṣad 4.3.7 and in the *Upadeśasāhasrī*, ch. 16. vv. 12-15 and ch. 18. v.152.). Śaṅkara argued that the revealer must be different from the revealed: the knower is other than what is known. In this verse the teacher says that there is no dispute between ourselves and the Buddhists in so far as we both accept that cognitions are known. The teacher then proceeds to argue, like Śaṅkara, that because the cognitions are known, i.e. because cognitions are "mental objects", they must be known by something other, namely the Awareness-Self. The teacher presents his argument as an inference: cognitions are known by something other, because of the fact that they are known, [for whenever a thing is known, it is known by something other], as in the case of sense-objects.

The teacher then argues:

परसंविदिताः सततं हि यतो न विदुः स्वममी विषयास्तु ततः ।
मतयोऽपि तथा परसंविदिता न विदुः स्वममूर्विषयास्तु यथा ॥१३॥

Because sense-objects are always known by something other, they do not know themselves. Likewise, the cognitions too are known by something other and do not know themselves, just as in the case of sense-objects. (13)

comment

In the preceding verse the teacher argued that when a thing becomes an object of knowledge it is always known by something other. In the present verse the teacher takes the argument a further step and says that when a thing is known by something other then it does not know itself. The idea is that when a thing is known or revealed as an object, then it is revealed by something other, and when a thing is revealed by something other, then it cannot be self-revealing. The argument is directed against the Buddhist teaching that a cognition is both the revealer and the revealed, it reveals itself and its content. The teacher says that cannot be so because a cognition is objectively present in the mind, it is something *known*, and since it is known it cannot be the knower.

Leaving the discussion of the Buddhist position, the teacher now explains the understanding of the mind according to Advaita in order to show that cognition is a function of the mind and the mind is revealed by the Awareness-Self.

विषयाकृतिसंस्थितिरेकविधा मनसस्तु सदा व्यवहारविधौ ।
अहमित्यपि तद्विषया त्वपरा मतिवृत्तिरवज्वलितात्मचिता ॥१४॥

It is always the case that in everyday life the mind has one type of cognition which takes on the form of the sense-object and it also has another cognition, "I", which has the first type as its object. [Both types of] cognition are illumined by the Awareness-Self. (14)

comment

In ordinary mental activity there are two types of cognition. The first is known as the *viṣayākāravṛtti*, or the cognition which takes on the form of the sense-object. That cognition alone is not sufficient to account for our ordinary mental activity, for we do not just have the cognition of the sense-object, such as "this is a tree". We can also think or say, "I see the tree". When we think or say "I", the tree cognition is the object of the "I". This "I" is called the *draṣṭrākāravṛtti*, the cognition which takes the form of the seer. This "I", or more correctly the "I"-thought *(ahaṁvṛtti)*, is also a mode of the mind. It is not the intrinsic Self because the "I"-thought is something known. Also, it is not always present, as in sleep, in moments of laughter and joy, and when the mind is deeply absorbed in some activity. Thus the "I" which is the subject of our everyday discourse, is not the essential Self but is a mode of the mind. Both types of cognition - the changing cognitions that represent the sense-objects, and the more permanent "I"-thought - are revealed by the Self, the absolute "Seer" or principle of illumination, the Self which is by nature just Awareness.

The teacher explains how the confusion between the ego "I" and the Self occurs.

पुरुषस्य तु धर्मवदुद्भवति स्वरसेन मतेः स्वगुणोऽपि यतः ।
अत आत्मगुणं प्रतियन्ति जना मतिवृत्तिमिमामहमित्यबुधाः ॥१५॥

Though [the "I"-thought] is inherently an attribute of the mind, it manifests as if it is an attribute of the Self. That is why ignorant people believe that this mode of the mind, "I", is an attribute of the Self. (15)

comment

The teacher points out that due to ignorance we mix up subject and object even though they are logically distinct. It is natural to believe that the "I"-thought is the Self because the "I"-thought seems to be innermost. But that is not so, because the "I"-thought is something known. Therefore it is not innermost. In order to reveal that the innermost Self is pure Awareness, the "I"-thought too is negated as the Self.

If the "I" is not the essential Self, does that mean that the "I" has to be suppressed? The teacher discusses this in the following five verses.

यदि सा न भवेज्जनमोहकरी व्यवहारमिमं न जनोऽनुभवेत् ।
विफलश्च तदा विषयानुभवो ज्ञगुणो न हि सेति यदा विदिता ॥१६॥

If that "I"-thought, which causes confusion in people, did not exist, people could not experience ordinary, transactional life. And the experience of sense-objects would be futile when the "I"-thought is understood as not an attribute of Awareness. (16)

comment

The teacher says that although the "I"-thought is an attribute of the mind, the existence of the "I"-thought is necessary in order to conduct the ordinary activities of life. The "I"-thought is present as the first person in such thoughts or statements as: "I think", "I see", "I am going", "I am thirsty" etc. If we suppress the first person singular then all such everyday dealings *(vyavahāra)* would be impossible, just as they are impossible for the yogī in *nirvikalpaka samādhi.* But Advaita is not the same as yoga. In Advaita, the false does not need to be suppressed, it just needs to be clearly seen for what it is. All the activities of life presuppose the superimposition between the Self and the body-sense-mind complex. Śaṅkara says that: "All epistemological activities, whether of a worldly or a Vedic nature, take place presupposing this mutual superimposition of the Self and the not-Self" (BSBh, *Adhyāsabhāṣya).* In other words the very structure of the cognising person is based upon superimposition, and this superimposition just needs to be understood for what it is, for then it is negated by knowledge. In the first sentence of the verse the teacher says that the "I"-thought need not be suppressed, it is necessary for transactional life. The "I"-thought must be known for what it is: the "I"-thought is the subject in everyday discourse and transactional life, but it should not be mistaken for the essential Self.

Furthermore, not only is the existence of the "I"-thought necessary for everyday life, but if the "I"-thought did not present itself as the Self, then "the experience of sense-objects would be futile", because there would be no point to experience if the Self and the experiencer are different. What the teacher says is that because there is the mutual superimposition of the mind and the Self, the mental modification in the form of "I" becomes sentient and the Self seems to become an experiencer. The Awareness-Self is the empirical experiencer by means of the superimposed "I"-thought. The experiencer, therefore, is not someone other than the Self.

The teacher elaborates as to why the "I"-thought has to be accepted as a part of the experience of everyday life.

उपलभ्यघटादिनिभैव भवेन्मनसो यदि संस्थितिरेकविधा ।
पुरुषस्य चितिश्च न विक्रियते मतिवृत्तिमपेक्ष्य घटादिनिभाम् ॥१७॥

If the mind has just one type of mode [that which takes on the form of the sense-object], and the Awareness pertaining to the Self does not undergo change with regard to the cognition presenting the object such as the pot etc., there would only be the cognition presenting the object, the pot and so forth. (17)

comment

If Awareness is changeless and the mind has only the cognition that takes on the form of the sense-object *(viṣayākāravṛtti),* but it does not have the cognition which takes the form of the seer *(draṣṭrākāravṛtti)*, then the cognition of a pot etc. would not be possible, because there would be no subject "I".

अवगन्त्रवगम्यचिदात्मधियोरहमित्यभिमानविहीनतया ।
स्थितयोरभिमानपुरःसरकं व्यवहारपथं न जनोऽवतरेत् ॥१८॥

If the Awareness-Self, the Knower, and the cognition, the known, were to remain without the ego-subject, the "I", then a person could not engage in the situations of ordinary life as they presuppose that ego-subject. (18)

अहमीक्ष इति प्रथमं हि धिया सुविचिन्त्य ततो विषयाभिमुखम् ।
नयनं प्रहिणोति तथान्यदपि श्रवणादि वियत्प्रमुखस्य गुणे ॥१९॥

Having first decided to look, a person directs his eye to the sense-object. In the same way, a person directs the other senses also, the ear etc., to the quality [of the corresponding element] beginning with space. (19)

comment

The teacher says that it is a matter of experience that the operation of the sense-organs depends upon the "I"-thought. Often there is the decision: "I shall see this", "I shall hear this" etc. and then a person directs the sense-organ to the relevant sense-object. Thus the activities of everyday life are impossible without the "I"-thought.

The statement that "a person directs the other senses also, the ear etc., to the quality [of the corresponding element] beginning with space" is peripheral to understanding the main argument. However what this expression refers to, is the teaching that the physical world consists of a mutual combination of five elements: space, air, fire, water and earth. The sense-organs are derived from these five elements while the elements are still in a subtle condition, before their mutual combination to form the gross physical world. The sense of hearing is formed from the subtle element space, the sense of touch is formed from the subtle element air, the sense of sight is formed from the subtle element fire, the sense of taste is formed from the subtle element water and the sense of smell is formed from the subtle element earth. Each sense-organ apprehends the particular quality residing in its corresponding element. Thus the sense of hearing apprehends sound which is the special quality of space, the sense of touch apprehends touch which is the special quality of air, the sense of sight apprehends form which is the special quality of the element fire, the sense of taste apprehends taste which is the special quality of water and the sense of smell apprehends smell which is the special quality of earth. Further information on this can be found in Vedānta manuals such as *Tattvabodha* and *Pancīkaraṇam.*

The teacher concludes this topic.

अपहाय न कश्चिदहङ्करणं व्यवहारमुपैति कदाचिदपि ।
उपपन्नतरा हि मतेस्तु ततो व्यवहारपथं प्रति कारणता ॥२०॥

No one ever acts in accord with the normal situations of life if they give up the "I". Therefore it is entirely correct to say that the mind [i.e. the "I"-thought] forms the basis of ordinary life. (20)

The teacher says that the committed seekers should investigate the nature of the "I"-thought for themselves.

चितिशक्तिगुणः किमहङ्करणं किमु बुद्धिगुणोऽथ भवेदुभयोः ।
इति चिन्त्यमिदं मनसानलसैरुपपत्तिभिरात्महितं यतिभिः ॥२१॥

Is the "I" an attribute of Awareness, or is it an attribute of the mind, or else is it an attribute of both Awareness and the mind? Ascetics who are diligent should investigate this, with appropriate reasoning, as it is for their own benefit. (21)

How should one reason? The teacher explains.,

**उपलभ्यमहङ्करणं न भवेत्पुरुषस्य गुणो यदि तर्हि भवेत् ।
गुणिरूपमथावयवं गुणिनो न विहाय गुणः पृथगस्ति यतः ॥२२॥**

If the "I" is an attribute of the Self, the "I" could not be experienced, because an attribute does not exist separately if it is apart from the substantive or the component of the substantive. (22)

comment

The reasoning is based upon the distinction between subject and object: whatever can be objectified is not identical to the subject. The teacher says that if the "I"-thought is an attribute of the Self then the "I"-thought would never be experienced. Why? Because a thing cannot be experienced unless it is objectified. If the attribute is to be experienced by the substantive, the attribute would have to stand in an objective relation to the substantive. But then the attribute would be separate from the substantive and it would thereby cease to exist because an attribute cannot exist separately from its substantive. A colour such as blue is always the attribute of some substantive, such as a cloth, or the components of the substantive such as the threads of the cloth. The colour cannot exist independently of the cloth or the threads. If the "I"-thought is an attribute of the Self, the "I"-thought could not be experienced by the Self unless it stands apart from the Self. But the "I"-thought could not exist apart from the Self. So if the "I"-thought is an attribute of the Self there is no way the "I"-thought could be experienced.

Perhaps the attribute can be experienced by the substantive, or by other attributes of the substantive, even while it remains in the substantive? The teacher says that cannot be so:

न गुणो गुणिनि स्थितवान् गुणिना विषयीक्रियते न च तस्य गुणैः ।
न हि देशकृता न च वस्तुकृता गुणिनोऽस्ति गुणस्य भिदा तु यतः ॥२३॥

An attribute residing in a substantive is not objectified by either the substantive or by the attributes of the substantive, for there is no separation of the attribute from the substantive, either spacewise or objectwise. (23)

comment

There is no separation between a substantive and its attribute and in the absence of separation there can be no subject-object relation and consequently there can be no experience of the attribute by the substantive. So if the "I"-thought is an attribute of the Self, the "I"-thought would not be experienced.

The teacher gives an example.

न परस्परमग्निगुणोऽग्निगतो विषयत्वमुपैति कदाचिदपि ।
न हि वह्निरपि स्वगुणं स्वगतं विषयीकुरुते स्वगुणेन भुवि ॥२४॥

An attribute [eg. the light] of fire never becomes an object of another attribute [eg. the heat] of fire and vice versa. Nor is it found that fire objectifies one of its attributes through another of its attributes. (24)

comment

Sureśvara says in his *Naiṣkarmyasiddhi:*

Just as the blazing fire does not burn its heat, since heat is its own nature, likewise the Self cannot know its "I", because there is no distinction. (2.23)

In the next eight verses the teacher refers to the Vaiśeṣika doctrine whose founder is said to be the sage Kaṇāda. The Vaiśeṣikas hold the view that the Self is the possessor of impermanent attributes such as happiness, sadness, desire, hatred, effort, virtue and vice. The teacher argues against this doctrine.

कणभुग्यमचीक्लृपदात्मगुणं गुणपूगमनित्यमनात्मगुणम् ।
अनयैव दिशा स निराक्रियतां न हि नित्यमनित्यगुणेन गुणि ॥२५॥

Kaṇāda has imagined a whole group of attributes which are impermanent and are [actually] attributes of the non-Self, to be the attributes of the Self. That entire group can be refuted in this same way [as shown above]. Indeed, no eternal entity becomes a substantive with an impermanent attribute. (25)

comment

Kaṇāda upholds the view that the Self is eternal and that it possesses attributes. We generally consider that states like happiness, sadness, desire, hatred etc. are attributes of the Self. But according to Advaita, they are attributes of the mind. The *Bṛhadāraṇyaka* Upaniṣad says: "desire, volition, doubt, faith, lack of faith, steadiness, unsteadiness, shyness, intelligence, fear - all these are but the mind." (1.5.3). The teacher says that the belief that these are attributes of the Self can be refuted by the same reasoning as before. The reasoning is that if these are attributes of the Self then they could not be experienced. Since happiness, sadness and so forth are in fact experienced, they must be other than the Self. Therefore these are states of the mind.

The last sentence of the verse gives an additional reason. Kaṇāda has said that the Self, which is eternal, has attributes like happiness, sadness etc. which are impermanent. The teacher says that we do not find an eternal entity having impermanent attributes. This point is taken up in the following verse.

If the followers of Kaṇāda are asked for an example of something eternal which has impermanent attributes, they reply that space is eternal and space has the impermanent attribute of sound. The teacher says that the example is wrong, because space is not eternal.

वियतः प्रभवं प्रवदन्ति यतः श्रुतयो बहुशः खमनित्यमतः ।
उपमानमनित्यगुणं वियतो न हि नित्यमिहास्ति कणादमते ॥२६॥

There are numerous statements in the Upaniṣads which state that space has an origin, therefore space is impermanent. In the doctrine of Kaṇāda there is no illustration, other than space, where an eternal entity has an impermanent attribute. (26)

comment

Taittirīya Upaniṣad 2.1.1, for example, speaks about the origin of space.

The follower of Vaiśeṣika then shifts the argument to another issue in order to prove the original point, namely that the Self has qualities. He asks about the relation between the Self and the mind. The Self is formless and the mind is a material entity. There has to be some connection between the Self and the mind and according to the Vaiśeṣikas, connection *(saṁyoga)* is an attribute. So by this argument the Vaiśeṣika again tries to show that the Self has attributes. The teacher answers this objection in the following three verses:

मनसा पुरुषः पुरुषेण मनो नभसा मुसलं मुसलेन नभः ।
न हि योगवियोगमुपैति कुतोऽवयवित्वनिराकरणादमुतः ॥२७॥

इह रज्जुघटादि हि सावयवं समुपैति युजामितरेतरतः ।
इति दृष्टमतोऽन्यददृष्टमपि स्वयमूह्यमिदं त्वपरित्यजता ॥२८॥

The Self is not connected to the mind nor is the mind connected to the Self, nor do they have a relation of disjunction. A pestle is not connected to space, nor is space connected to the pestle, nor do they have a relation of disjunction. Why? Because of the denial that [the Self and space] possess parts. (27)

It is observed that a rope and a pot etc., all of which have parts, can be joined to each other. You can infer this for yourself about any other thing, even if you have not seen it, provided you do not forget what you have observed. (28)

comment

The teacher says that on the basis of personal observation we can see that only things having parts can become connected. A pot, for example, can be joined to a rope and vice versa. Anything that has parts can be connected to another thing which has parts. The teacher says that a person can inductively infer this to be true.

न हि सावयवं विगतावयवैर्विगतावयवं च न सावयवैः ।
उपयाति युजामिति दृष्टमिदं यत एवमतः स्थितमुक्तमदः ॥२९॥

It is seen that a thing having parts is not joined to things that are without parts, and a thing that is without parts is not joined to things having parts. That being so, what we said before holds good. (29)

comment

Things with parts can enter into a relation of connection or disjunction with other things having parts. But something having parts cannot be joined to something without parts and vice versa. A pestle, for example, cannot be joined to space which is without parts, nor can the latter be joined to the pestle. Since they cannot be connected there can be no relation of disjunction *(viyoga)* between them. Similarly, the Self is not seen to have any parts, therefore the Self does not have a relation of connection with the mind. So what was said before in verse twenty seven is established.

On the principle of "driving in the post" *(sthūnānikhanananyāya)*, i.e. adding additional arguments to further strengthen what one has already said, the teacher takes up a possible objection and dismisses it in the following verse.

न हि कल्पितभागसमागमनं विगतावयवस्य घटेत कुतः ।
वितथत्वमतिः सुदृढा तु यतः परिकल्पितवस्तुषु नित्यमतः ॥३०॥

Something without parts cannot possibly have a connection with parts that have been superimposed. Why? Because of the firm understanding that things that are superimposed are always unreal. (30)

In the following two verses the teacher concludes the discussion with the Vaiśeṣika begun in verse twenty-five.

इह वेदशिरःसु तदर्थविदः प्रवदन्ति समस्तजगत्प्रकृतिम् ।
परमात्मपदं दृशिमात्रवपुर्ध्रुवमेकमतोऽन्यदनित्यमिति ॥३१॥

अत एव न किञ्चिदुदाहरणं ध्रुवमस्ति परस्य विनाशिगुणम् ।
यत एवमतः स्थितमुक्तमदो न हि नित्यमनित्यगुणेन गुणि ॥३२॥

Here, at the apex of the Veda (i.e. in the Upaniṣads), those who know the meaning of those Upaniṣads say that the supreme Self is the material cause of the entire world, that the supreme Self is in the form of mere Seeing [Awareness], that It is permanent and one. Anything other than that is impermanent. (31)

Therefore the opponent, i.e the Vaiśeṣika, has no illustration of a permanent entity having an impermanent attribute. Since this is so, what we said before holds good: "no eternal entity becomes a substantive with an impermanent attribute". (32)

The teacher now returns to the topic begun in verse twenty-one, whether the "I"-thought is an attribute of the Self or an attribute of the mind.

उपलभ्यमहङ्करणं भवितुं क्षमते दृशिरूपगुणो न यतः ।
विषयाकृतिरञ्जितधीगुणवद् विषयत्वमहङ्करणस्य ततः ॥३३॥

Since the "I" is able to be experienced, it is not an attribute of Seeing [Awareness]. Hence the "I" has the status of an object, like the cognition that takes on the form of the sense-object. (33)

comment

This verse presents the conclusive Advaita teaching, namely that the ego or "I"-thought is not an attribute of the Self for the reason that the "I"-thought can be objectified. Since the "I" is something known, it is not identical to the Knower. The Knower is, ultimately, nothing other than pure Awareness. The "I"-thought is an object and so it is an attribute of the mind, similar to the cognition which represents the form of the sense-object *(viṣayākāravṛtti).* In verse fourteen it was said that the mind has two types of cognition: the cognition which takes on the form of the sense-object and the cognition which presents itself as the transactional subject, i.e. the "I"-thought.

The teacher now presents the definitive Advaita understanding about the Self and the mind.

विषयप्रकृतिं प्रतिपन्नवतीं मतिवृत्तिमहङ्करणं च मतेः ।
उभयं परिपश्यति योऽविकृतः परमात्मसदुक्तिरसौ पुरुषः ॥३४॥

The One who, without undergoing change, sees both these: the cognition which takes on the form of the sense-object and brings about the apprehension of the object, and the mental property "I"; - that Self is called the "supreme Self" *(paramātmā)* and "Being itself" [Brahman] *(sat).* (34)

comment

This important verse presents the conclusive position of Advaita with regard to the nature of the mind and the understanding of the Self

The mind has two types of cognition: the first consists of the various cognitions that apprehend the sense-object *(viṣayākāravṛtti)* and the second consists of the notion of "I", the ego or "I"-thought *(draṣṭrākāravṛtti).* The latter is the subject of everyday activities such as thinking, desiring, willing, remembering and doing etc. If the "I" is not the essential Self, what then is the essential Self? The essential Self is the luminous Seeing, or Awareness, which does not change and which illumines both the ego and the cognitions which reveal the world.

Verses six through to thirty-three were primarily concerned with clarifying the understanding of the essential Self. Verse thirty-four directly states that this Self is none other than That which is expressed by such words as "Brahman" etc.

The student now expresses a doubt with reference to what has just been said and the teacher replies to him.

ननु देहभृदेष कथं भवताभिहितः परमात्मसदुक्तिरिति ।
न विरुद्धमवादिषमेतदहं श्रुतिरप्यमुमर्थमुवाच यतः ॥३५॥

[student]: How can you say that this embodied Self is the "supreme Self" and "Brahman"? [teacher]: I have not said anything contradictory, for the *śruti* too has told this meaning. (35)

The teacher cites a number of passages from the *śruti.*

अमतं न मतेरमतस्तदिदं यदमुत्र तदेव तु कश्चिदिति ।
श्रुतिषु प्रतिपादितमस्य दृशेः परमात्मपदत्वममूषु भृशम् ॥३६॥

"Not thought [It is the Thinker]"; "[you cannot think the Thinker] of thought"; "[the Thinker who is] not thought"; "that [Brahman is without before and after, without interior and exterior]"; "[all] this [which exists, is this Self]"; "what [is here] is There, [what is There] is likewise [here]";

"some [wise person...saw the inner-Self]". In these *śrutis* it is repeatedly taught that this Seeing is the Supreme Self. (36)

comment

The teacher cites words from a number of passages in the *Bṛhadāraṇyaka* Upaniṣad: "This Immutable, O Gārgī, is not seen, It is the Seer; It is not heard, It is the Hearer; It is not thought, It is the Thinker; It is not known, It is the Knower. There is no other seer than This, there is no other hearer than This, there is no other thinker than This, there is no other knower than This..." (3.8.11). "You cannot see the Seer of seeing; one cannot hear the Hearer of hearing, you cannot think the Thinker of thought, you cannot know the Knower of knowing" (3.4.2). "The Seer who is not seen, the Hearer who is not heard, the Thinker who is not thought, the Knower who is not known. There is no other seer than This, there is no other hearer than This, there is no other thinker than This, there is no other knower than This..." (3.7.23). "That Brahman is without before and after, without interior and exterior" (2.5.19). "This Brāhmaṇa, this Kṣatriya, these worlds, these gods, these Vedas, these beings - all this which exists - is this Self" (4.5.7).

The teacher also cites from the *Kaṭha* Upaniṣad: "What is here is There and what is There is likewise here. He who sees the as though many here goes from death to death" (2.1.10). "The self-existent Lord made the external senses worthless. Therefore one sees external things and not the inner-Self. Some wise person, desirous of immortality, turned his eyes away [from external things] and saw the inner-Self" (2.1.1).

Now the teacher refers to the *Kena* Upaniṣad.

यदनभ्युदितं वदनेन सदा नयनेन च पश्यति यन्न सदा ।
श्रवणेन च यन्न शृणोति सदा मनसापि च यन्मनुते न सदा ॥३७॥

वदनं नयनं च तथा श्रवणं मन एव च येन मतं सततम् ।
अवगच्छ तदेव पदं परमं त्वमिति श्रुतिरीक्षितुरुक्तवती ॥३८॥

It is never expressed by speech. A person never sees It with the eye. A person never hears It with the ear and with the mind never thinks It. (37)

You must understand the supreme Self to be That through Which speech, sight, hearing and the mind itself are always known. Thus has the *śruti* instructed the prepared student. (38)

comment

These two verses refer to a series of passages in the *Kena* Upaniṣad (1.5-8.). Verse thirty-seven gives the meaning of the first part of each of those passages and verse thirty-eight presents the meaning of the rest of each passage. The passages from the *Kena* Upaniṣad are: "That which is not spoken by speech, That by which speech is spoken. You should understand That to be Brahman. Not this which people meditate upon as an object" (1.5.). "A person does not think which with the mind, That by which, they say, the mind is thought. You should understand That to be Brahman. Not this which people meditate upon as an object" (1.6.). "That which a person does not see with the eye, That by which one sees the eyes. You should understand That to be Brahman. Not this which people meditate upon as an object" (1.7). "That which a person does not hear with the ear, That by which this hear is heard. You should understand That to be Brahman. Not this which people meditate upon as an object" (1.8.).

These *śruti* texts directly indicate that the Self is Brahman. The method here is twofold. Firstly, the *śruti* negates the idea that Brahman can be an object of either language, the senses, or the mind. This is the meaning of the first part of each of the passages. But the *śruti* does not then become silent, because if the *śruti* merely said that Brahman exists, but Brahman cannot be known, the consequence would be that any further Upaniṣad teaching would be worthless. In the remaining portion of the passages the *śruti* gives the second part of the twofold method in which it positively indicates Brahman through implication *(lakṣaṇā).* The *śruti* said that Brahman is not expressed though speech, i.e. Brahman is not the direct object of any word. But the *śruti* then proceeds to directly reveal Brahman through words: "That by which speech is spoken", "That by which the mind is thought" etc. The *śruti,* while recognising the inherent limitations of language, nonetheless uses language to communicate

Brahman, for there is no other way for the *śruti* to communicate Brahman. The *śruti* can communicate Brahman through language when (a) the context has been made clear through the previous negation, and (b) because Brahman is immediately present *(aparokṣa)* as the very Self of the speaker, thinker, seer and hearer. The *śruti* cannot reveal Brahman as the direct object of a word. However the *śruti* directly reveals that the "inner" Awareness is Brahman through words functioning by way of implication. This is what occurs in these statements: "That by which speech is spoken", "That by which the mind is thought", "That by which one sees the eyes" and "That by which this hearing is heard"; where the phrase "by which" is used to directly indicate Brahman. The implied meaning of the "by which" is then pointed out to be Brahman: "You should understand That to be Brahman".

परमात्मपदत्व इयं च मया श्रुतिरल्पकणोक्तिरिहाभिहिता ।
अणिमादिगुणं सदिति प्रकृतं तदसि त्वमिति श्रुतिरभ्यवदत् ॥३९॥

In this matter of one's being the supreme Self, I have only cited very small portions of the *śruti.* [In the *Chāndogya* Upaniṣad] Being Itself, with the attributes such as having the greatest subtlety etc, is the subject matter, and the *śruti* has stated: "you are That"! (39)

comment

In response to the question raised in verse thirty-five, the teacher referred to a number of *śruti* statements to show that the *śruti* teaches that the "inner"-Awareness is none other than the absolute reality called by such terms as "supreme Self" or "pure Being". These were but brief *śruti* quotations. In this verse the teacher refers to chapter six of the *Chāndogya* Upaniṣad where Āruṇi teaches his son Śvetaketu the nature of Brahman and then repeatedly tells him: "you are That" *(tattvamasi).*

The teacher negates the idea that the Self could perhaps be just a part of the supreme Self or a modification of the supreme Self.

नभसोऽवयवो विकृतिश्च यथा घटिकादिनभो न भवेत्तु तथा ।
परमात्मन एष न चावयवो विकृतिश्च शरीरभृदित्यमृषा ॥४०॥

Just as the space within a pot etc. can neither be a part of space nor a modification of space, so too, this embodied Self can neither be a part nor a modification of the supreme Self. So [what I have told you] is not wrong. (40)

comment

One may believe that the embodied Self is a part of Brahman or is a modification of Brahman. The teacher says it is not so. To explain this he uses the analogy of space. The space contained within a pot is not a part of the total space, nor is it a modification of space. The space within the pot is identical to the space outside the pot. The seeming difference between the space within the pot and the space outside the pot is brought about just by the form of the pot. Thus the difference of space as being "inside" and "outside" is dependent upon the pot. There is no distinction within space itself. Similarly, the embodied Self is neither a part of Brahman nor a modification of Brahman, but is Brahman Itself.

If there is no difference at all between the Self and Brahman, then what is meant by the term "individual self" *(jīva)?*

करकादिनिमित्तकमेव यथा करकाम्बरनाम भवेद्वियतः ।
परमात्मदृशेरपि नाम तथा पुरहेतुकमेव तु जीव इति ॥४१॥

As space can have the designation of "pot-space" just on account of the pot etc., so too, the supreme Self, the Seeing, acquires the designation "individual soul" *(jīva)* just because of the body. (41)

comment

Though space is indivisible, we can speak of "pot-space", "room-space" etc. These divisions are not intrinsic to space but are dependent upon the limiting adjuncts *(upādhi)*, the form of the pot and the walls of the room. All difference between space is thus made by limiting adjuncts which seem to delimit space. The teacher says that the situation is similar in regard to Brahman, the Seeing, or Awareness. As mentioned in the comment to verse seven, difference is created only by limiting adjuncts. When Brahman is apparently conditioned by the body-sense-mind complex, then Brahman is called the individual soul or *jīva*.

Furthermore, the statements in the *śruti* about the "entry" of the supreme Self into the manifested world show that the individual self is neither a part nor a modification of the supreme Self, but is directly the supreme Self.

जनितं वियदग्रणि येन जगत्परमात्मसदक्षरनामभृता ।
प्रविवेश स एव जगत्स्वकृतं खमिवेह घटं घटसृष्टिमनु ॥४२॥

That One, who is referred to by such names as the "supreme Self" *(paramātmā)*, "Being" *(sat)*, "Immutable" *(akṣara)*, produced the world beginning with the element space. It is He who entered the world that He created, like space enters a pot even as the pot is created. (42)

comment

There are a number of *śruti* statements describing the "entry" of the supreme Self into the world. For example, the *Bṛhadāraṇyaka* Upaniṣad says: "This [world] was then unmanifest. It manifested only as name-and-form....The Self entered here [into these bodies] up to the tip of the nails" (1.4.7). In the *Taittirīya* Upaniṣad it is said: "He desired, 'I will be many, I will be born'. He undertook deliberation and having deliberated he projected everything, whatever exists. Having projected the world He entered into that very world" (2.6.1). The statement that Brahman has "entered" the world is metaphorical, as is the statement about the entry of space into the created pot. Space does not "enter" the pot; once the pot is created it seems to delimit the ever-present space. Similarly, the manifestation of the world of name-and-form seems to delimit Brahman, but Brahman does not literally "enter" into the world because an entry implies the movement of a finite thing from one place to another.

The verse says that there is no separate individual self who is a part or a modification of Brahman. Brahman, when apparently conditioned by a particular *upādhi*, is the "individual self" in relation to that *upādhi*. Thus individuality is dependent upon the *upādhi*, it is not intrinsic. There is only one Self in all beings, Brahman.

The teacher says that even the *śruti* statements that speak about the creation of the world are only meant to reveal oneness.

उदपद्यत खप्रमुखं हि जगत्परमात्मन इत्यपि याः श्रुतयः ।
अवधार्यत आभिरभेदमतिः परमात्मसतत्त्वसमर्पणतः ॥ ४३॥

Non-difference is ascertained even from those *śrutis* which tell that the world beginning with space arose from the supreme Self. For what they convey is that [the world and the individual soul] have the same essential nature as the supreme Self. (43)

comment

The purport of the *śruti* passages to do with creation is to show two things. Firstly, that the "name-and-form", i.e. the material which comprises the physical world, is non-separate from Brahman. Secondly, the *śruti* tells that Brahman "entered" into the manifested world as the Self of all the diverse living forms.

यदि सृष्टिविधानपरं वचनं फलशून्यमनर्थकमेव भवेत् ।
जगदित्थमजायत धातुरिति श्रवणं पुरुषस्य फलाय न हि ॥४४॥

If the statements [which speak about the origin of the world] are meant to describe the way in which the world is created, they would be of no benefit and would prove to be worthless. Hearing how the world arose from the creator is of no benefit to a person. (44)

comment

The teacher says that the statements in the *śruti* which speak of the creation (or to convey the Sanskrit term *sṛṣṭi* more accurately: the "projection" or "emission") of the world of name-and-form from the creator do not have their purport in describing how the world came about. The *śruti* does not have its purport in stating that space was the first element to arise, followed by air, fire, water and earth. These details are not the purport of the *śruti.* Their purport is in teaching that the world of name-and-form has no separate existence from Brahman and in teaching that Brahman is the Self of all beings. Knowing how the world arose is not beneficial because it is not a liberating knowledge, it is just another piece of knowledge, or, more accurately, information, to add to the stock of already accumulated information. This additional information does not liberate a person from sorrow, for the person remains the same as before, plus the additional information. However the understanding that everything is Brahman does have a result, for it has the capacity to liberate the person from sorrow by removing the erroneous notions of self.

अनृतत्वमवादासकृद्विकृतेर्निरधारि सदेव तु सत्यमिति ।
श्रुतिभिर्बहुधैतदतोऽवगतं जगतो न हि जन्म विधेयमिति ॥४५॥

The *śrutis* have repeatedly stated, in a variety of ways, that modifications are unreal whereas they have ascertained that Brahman alone is real. Therefore it is understood that the origin of the world is not what is meant to be described. (45)

comment

Furthermore, the origin of the world cannot be the purport of the *śruti* texts which speak of creation, for the *śruti* repeatedly tells that the world of name-and-form is unreal *(anṛta i.e. mithyā)* and that Brahman alone is real *(satya)*. For example, in the sixth chapter of the *Chāndogya* Upaniṣad it is said repeatedly that: "a modification is a name having its origin in language *(vācārambhaṇaṁ vikāro nāmadheyam)*." The idea is that a thing has no reality of its own separate from its material cause. This will be explained in detail later on. That Upaniṣad also repeatedly stated that Brahman alone is real: "That is the subtle essence which everything has as its Self. That is real That is the Self. You are That, Śvetaketu!" (6.8.7.ff.)

न च तत्त्वमसीत्यसकृद्वचनं जगतो जनिमात्रविधौ घटते ।
परमात्मपदानुमतिं तु यदा जनयेत्पुरुषस्य तदा घटते ॥४६॥

The repeated statement "you are That" cannot be about the mere origination of the world. But when the statement "you are That" makes a person understand the essential identity with the supreme Self, then [a statement to do with the origin of the world] fits in [as a subsidiary]. (46)

comment

The *śruti* statements about the origination of the world are meant to assist the understanding of oneness, they are not just to provide a description of the process of creation. In the sixth chapter of the *Chāndogya* Upaniṣad there are statements about creation and there is the *mahāvākya "tat tvam asi"*. In this verse the teacher says that the student should not suppose that the statement *"tattvamasi"* could be subordinate to the statements about creation. The primary importance of the *mahāvākya* is shown by the fact that it is repeated nine times. This repetition is appropriate because that *mahāvākya* produces the beneficial liberating knowledge. But statements about creation have no such benefit and so if the *mahāvākya* was subordinate to statements about creation the repetition would be incongruous. The statements teaching identity are the primary purport of the *śruti* and statements about the origination of the world are subordinate to the teaching of identity. Statements about the origin of the world are meant to assist the knowledge of identity by showing that the world of name-and-form is not separate from Brahman.

स्थिरजङ्गमदेहधियां चरितं परिपश्यति योऽविकृतः पुरुषः ।
परमात्मसदुक्तिरसाविति यद्गणितं तदतिष्ठिपमित्थमहम् ॥४७॥

Thus I have established what I said before, namely that the One who, without undergoing change, sees the activity of the minds of living beings whether they are stationary or moving - that Self is called the "supreme Self" *(paramātmā)* and "Being itself" [Brahman] *(sat).* (47)

comment

In verse thirty-four the teacher said that the Witness-Self is none other than That which is expressed by such words as "supreme Self and "Brahman" etc. In verse thirty-five, the student questioned the possibility of what the teacher had said. In verses thirty-six to thirty-nine the teacher cited the *śruti* as the means of knowledge *(pramāṇa)* for what he had said. In verse forty he argued against the idea that the inner-Self could be either a part or a modification of Brahman and in verse forty-one he explained that Brahman acquires the designation of "individual soul" *(jīva)* just because of limiting adjuncts *(upādhi).* In verse forty-two the teacher cited the *śruti* as saying that, following creation, Brahman itself "entered" the world as the individual soul. In verses forty-three to forty-six he explained that the statements to do with creation are only meant to assist the teaching of identity. In the present verse the teacher restates the conclusive position expressed in verse thirty-four.

The teacher then supports his conclusion with an additional reason.

पृथगेव यदाक्षरतो मतिविन्मकरोदक्वन्न घटाम्बरवत् ।
न विरोत्स्यति तत्त्वमसीति तदा वचनं कथमेष त इत्यपि च ॥४८॥

If the Knower of the mind is really separate from the Immutable [Brahman], like a fish is separate from water - unlike the pot-space - how will it not contradict the statement "you are That" and the statement "This is your Self"? (48)

comment

If there is a real difference between the Self and Brahman, like there is a real difference between the fish and the water in which it swims - unlike the example of the non-difference of the pot-space from space - then this difference would directly contradict the statement of the *Chāndogya* Upaniṣad: "you are That" (6.8.7ff.), as well as the statement from the *Bṛhadāraṇyaka* Upaniṣad: "This is your Self" (3.7.3ff).

The student takes up this last point and raises an objection.

न तु वस्तुसतत्त्वविबोधनकृद्विनिवर्तयदप्रतिबोधमिदम् ।
सदुपासनकर्मविधानपरं यत एवमतो न विरोत्स्यति मे ॥४९॥

This sentence *[tattvamasi]* does not reveal the actual nature of Reality which removes ignorance. It is meant to prescribe an action consisting of a conceptual meditation upon Brahman. So, according to me, [the acceptance of difference] will not contradict [the statement *tattvamasi].* (49)

comment

The teacher argued that if there is a real difference between the Self and Brahman, the *śruti* statements such as "you are That" and "This is your Self" would be contradicted. The student says there need be no contradiction, because these *śruti* statements do not communicate the non-difference between the Self and Brahman. They are just meant in the context of a conceptual mediation, where the person performs a meditation wherein he imagines himself as Brahman.

The student further explains his objection.

मनआदिषु कारणदृष्टिविधिः प्रतिमासु च देवधियां करणम् ।
स्वमतिं ह्यनपोह्य यथा तु तथा त्वमसीह सदात्ममतिर्वचनात् ॥५०॥

Just as a person is enjoined to cultivate a conceptual meditation that the mind etc. are the Cause [i.e. Brahman] and just as a person looks upon images with the idea that they are the deities, all the while not relinquishing his understanding [that the mind is not the same as Brahman and that images are not the same as the deities], similarly, from the statement "you are That" [a person is enjoined to perform a conceptual meditation with] the idea that the Self is identical to Brahman. (50)

comment

Various conceptual meditations *(upāsanā)* are mentioned at different places in the *śruti* as a part of the mental training of the student. In the *Chāndogya* Upaniṣad there is the meditation: "one should meditate upon the mind as Brahman" and "one should meditate upon space as Brahman" (3.18.1). Also, after a stone-image is consecrated for worship it is looked upon as the form of the deity and treated as if it were the deity. But the worshipper does not relinquish his understanding that the image is made of stone. Similarly, the statement *"tattvamasi"* is just meant as a type of meditation to facilitate concentration of the mind and for any other result as promised by the *śruti.*

In the following two verses the student furnishes three other possible ways of understanding the sentence *"tat tvam asi".*

अथ वा त्वमिति ध्वनिवाच्यमिदं सदसीति वदेद्वचनं गुणतः ।
विभयं पुरुषं प्रवदन्ति यथा मृगराडयमीश्वरगुप्त इति ॥५१॥

Alternatively, this sentence *[tattvamasi]* could say metaphorically to the person expressed by the word "you" that "you are Brahman". It would be analogous to how people talk about a fearless person when they say: "this fellow, Īśvaragupta, is a lion!" (51)

comment

If the statement *"tattvamasi"* is not meant as a type of meditation, then perhaps it is just a metaphor as when we say about a brave person: "he is a lion!"

यदि वा स्तुतये सदसीति वदेन्मघवानसि विष्णुरसीति यथा ।
त्वमिति श्रुतिवाच्यसतत्त्वकतामथ वा सत एव वदेद्वचनम् ॥५२॥

Alternatively, [the sentence] could say "you are That" as a way of praising [the individual self], just as [people who are the recipients of gifts from a munificent person could praise that person saying:] "you are Indra!" "You are Viṣṇu!" Or else, the sentence might be saying that Brahman has actually acquired the nature of an individual soul who is expressed in the *śruti* by the word "you". (52)

comment

The statement *"tattvamasi"* could be just a form of eulogy, as when the receiver of a gift may say to the giver: "you are Viṣṇu!". Alternatively, the sentence *"tattvamasi"* may have the reverse meaning. Instead of saying "you are That", it may mean "That is you". In other words, instead of revealing that the individual self is Brahman, the statement could be saying that Brahman has become a *jīva,* i.e. Brahman has actually become a *saṁsārī.*

The student makes a final point.

यदि तत्त्वमिति ध्वनिनाभिहितः परमात्मसतत्त्वक एव सदा ।
किमिति स्वकमेष न रूपमवेत्प्रतिबोध्यत एव यतो वचनैः ॥५३॥

If the individual soul, who is expressed by the word "you" in the sentence *"tattvamasi"*, is always of the nature of the supreme Self, then why does the individual soul not know its own inherent nature? For we find that this inherent nature is only revealed by the *śruti* statements. (53)

comment

If the Self is really Brahman, then why is this fact not automatically known? Why should there be the requirement of the *śruti* to reveal this fact?

The student concludes.

अत एव हि जीवसदात्मकतां न हि तत्त्वमसीति वदेद्वचनम् ।
यदपीदृशमन्यदतो वचनं तदपि प्रथयेदनयैव दिशा ॥५४॥

Therefore the sentence *"tattvamasi"* would not say that the individual soul is identical to Brahman. So one should construe any other similar statement in this same way [as has been shown above]. (54)

comment

Any other statements in the *śruti* which express the identity between the individual soul and Brahman should be understood in any of the above four ways: (1) as a type of conceptual meditative practice, (2) as a metaphor, (3) as a way of praising the individual, or, (4) as teaching the opposite meaning, namely that Brahman has become a *saṁsārijīva*.

The teacher now commences his reply.

त्वदुदाहृतवाक्यविलक्षणता वचनस्य हि तत्त्वमसीति यतः ।
अत एव न दृष्टिविधानपरं सत एव सदात्मकतागमकम् ॥५५॥

The sentence *"tattvamasi"* is different to the sentences you have cited, so it is not meant to prescribe a conceptual meditation. It makes known that the Being [which is the essential nature of the individual soul] is identical to Brahman. (55)

comment

The student argued that a *mahāvākya,* such as *tattvamasi,* should be interpreted in any of the four ways described above. In addition, he raised the objection that if the Self is already Brahman then what is the need of the *śruti* to reveal this fact? The teacher replies to these five points up until verse 107, though the dialogue continues as the student responds to what the teacher is saying.

In this verse the teacher begins by saying that it is not correct to equate the different types of statements in the *śruti.* The statements in the *Chāndogya* Upaniṣad that: "one should meditate upon the mind as Brahman", "one should meditate upon space as Brahman" (3.18.1.) and "he meditates upon the sun as Brahman" (3.19.4.) etc., are of a completely different type from the statement *"tattvamasi".* Statements of the former type do not deal with reality, they are intended as a conceptual meditative practice to assist the development of concentration and mental focus on the part of the student, or they are enjoined to gain some particular result. Statements such as *"tattvamasi",* however, have a different aim, for they are meant as a direct revelation that one's own Being is Brahman.

इतिशब्दशिरस्कपदोक्तमतिर्विहिता मनआदिषु तैर्वचनैः ।
न विधानमिहास्ति तथा वचने सुविलक्षणमेतदतो वचनात् ॥५६॥

The sentences [such as "one should meditate upon the mind as Brahman" etc.] enjoin that the words mind etc. should take on the idea expressed by the word ending with the particle *iti.* But there is no such injunction here in the sentence *[tattvamasi].* So this sentence is entirely different to those. (56)

comment

In each of these sentences: "one should meditate upon the mind as Brahman" *(mano brahma iti upāsīta)*, "one should meditate upon space as Brahman" *(ākāśo brahma iti upāsīta)*, "he meditates upon the sun as Brahman" *(ādityaṁ brahma iti upāste)*, the word Brahman is followed by the specifying particle *iti*. These sentences enjoin a conceptual meditation in which the words "mind", "space", and "sun" are to be looked upon as Brahman *(brahma iti)*. The sentence asks the person to imagine that the mind is Brahman, to imagine that space is Brahman, and to imagine the sun as Brahman. The sentence *"tattvamasi"* is entirely different. It does not ask a person to imaginatively equate one thing [X] with something else [Y]. It is merely an indicative statement: you *are* That.

मनसो वियतः सवितृप्रभृतेः प्रवदन्ति न तानि सदात्मकताम् ।
मनआदि हि मुख्यमुपास्यतया प्रवदन्ति यतोऽक्षरदृष्टियुतम् ॥५७॥

Those sentences ["one should meditate upon the mind as Brahman" etc.] do not say that the mind, space, and the sun etc. are Brahman. What they say is that the words mind etc., understood just in their literal sense, are to be connected conceptually with the Immutable as a type of meditation. (57)

comment

The sentences such as "one should meditate upon the mind as Brahman" etc. merely tell the student to look upon the mind as Brahman, or to look upon space as Brahman, or to look upon the sun as Brahman. The words "mind", "space" and "sun" are not understood in any secondary sense, they are meant to be understood literally. So these sentences, when understood literally, are close to absurd because it is evident that the mind is not what is meant by Brahman, nor space, nor the sun. These sentences are therefore meant as part of a conceptual meditation, they are not meant as a revelation of reality, as is the case with *"tattvamasi"*.

The teacher raises a hypothetical objection and answers it.

करको न मृदः पृथगस्ति यथा मनआदि सतोऽस्ति तथा न पृथक् ।
इति वस्तुसतत्त्वकता तु यदा विधिशब्द इतिश्च तदा तु वृथा ॥५८॥

Just as an earthen pot is not separate from clay, so too the mind etc. are not separate from Brahman. If in this way [you think that these sentences] pertain to the true nature of reality, [we say] then the word expressing an injunction as well as the particle *"iti"* would serve no purpose. (58)

comment

The teacher argued that the *mahāvākya* such as *tattvamasi* and the sentences such as "one should meditate upon the mind as Brahman" are entirely different types of sentences, the former is meant to reveal reality while the latter are intended as a conceptual meditation. The teacher then says to the student: suppose you reverse your position and argue that if *"tattvamasi"* is accepted as revealing the true nature of reality, then all the other sentences such as "one should meditate upon the mind as Brahman" should also be accepted as revealing the true nature of reality, because what these sentences say is that the mind etc. have no separate existence from Brahman, just like an earthen pot has no separate existence from the clay. The teacher replies to this hypothetical objection by saying that if that is the case, then there would be no need for the injunctive verb or the particle *"iti"*. In the sentences such as "one should meditate upon the mind as Brahman" there is the injunction that "one should meditate" *(upāsīta)*, which commands the hearer to do something. There is also the particle *"iti"* which specifies what is laid down by the command. These sentences cannot be understood as just revealing a fact because they command that some type of mental action be performed. Therefore they must be different from the indicative sentence *tattvamasi.*

मनआदि समानविभक्तितया विधिशब्दमितिं च विहाय यदि ।

जनकेन सता सह योगमियादनृतं तदिति स्फुटमुक्तमभूत् ॥५९॥

If you were to remove the word expressing the injunction as well as the particle *iti*, the words mind etc. would be connected to Brahman, the Cause, through grammatical apposition. Then it would be clearly said that the mind is unreal. (59)

comment

The teacher says that if it is accepted that the injunctive words "one should meditate" and the particle *"iti"* serve no purpose and so we ignore them, then the words "mind" and "Brahman" would be directly equated due to the two terms having grammatical apposition. The two terms would then be co-referential *(samānādhikaraṇa)* and the sentence would mean that "mind is Brahman". But mind, understood literally, cannot be the same as Brahman. For if the mind is one real entity and Brahman is another real entity then the two real things cannot be equated. We cannot equate a table and a chair merely by saying: "a table is a chair." Therefore in order for the sentence to be meaningful we have to give up the reality of one of the terms. We can say, for example, "the table is wood", because in this case the table is not seen as a separate reality apart from wood. So if the sentence is saying that "mind is Brahman", what it is saying is that the mind has no independent existence apart from Brahman and therefore the mind is unreal *(mithyā)*.

The student raises a counter-objection.

ननु जीवसतोरपि तत्त्वमिति स्फुटमेकविभक्त्यभिधानमिदम् ।
कथमस्य शरीरभृतोऽनृतता न भवेदविभक्तविभक्तियुजः ॥६०॥

Well, the words *tat* and *tvam* [in the sentence *"tattvamasi"]* clearly show that grammatical apposition also exists between the individual soul and Brahman. So how can this embodied Self, who is in a relation of grammatical apposition, not be unreal? (60)

comment

The student says that if the apposition between the words "mind and "Brahman" reveals that the mind is unreal, then in the sentence *tattvamasi* the grammatical apposition between the two words "you" and "Brahman" should reveal that the individual soul is unreal.

The teacher replies in the following seven verses.

प्रकृतेरभिधानपदेन यदा विकृतेरभिधानमुपैति युजाम् ।
अनृतत्वमतिस्तु तदा विकृतौ मृदयं घट इत्यभिधासु यथा ॥६१॥

When a word denoting a product is connected to a word denoting its material cause then there is the understanding that the product is unreal. As in the case of expressions like "this pot is clay". (61)

comment

If one thing is the material cause and another thing is the product of that material cause, and the words which denote those things are seen to be co-referential in a sentence, then the sentence conveys the meaning that the product is unreal. As for example in the case of sentences such as: "the table is wood", or "the pot is clay". In these sentences the products, the table and the pot, are unreal in so far as they have no existence of their own apart from the existence of their respective material causes.

विकृतित्वमवादि मनःप्रभृतेर्बहुशः श्रुतिषु प्रकृतेस्तु सतः ।
अत एव समानविभक्तितया मनआदि सुवेद्यमसत्यमिति ॥६२॥

The *śrutis* have said on many occasions that the mind and so forth are products of Brahman, their material cause. And so, due to the grammatical apposition, it can be easily understood that the mind etc. are not real. (62)

comment

There are a number of *śruti* passages which reveal that the mind and everything else that makes up the physical world have originated from Brahman. For example, the *Muṇḍaka* Upaniṣad says: "From this [Puruṣa, i.e. Brahman] arises the *prāṇa*, the mind and all the senses..." (2.1.3). The following passage from the *Chāndogya* Upaniṣad says that mind is a modification of food which has originated from Brahman: "When food is eaten it becomes divided three ways. The gross element turns into excrement, the more subtle constituent becomes flesh and the most subtle portion becomes mind" (6.5.1). If we know that mind is the product and Brahman is its material cause, and if we see that mind and Brahman are used in a sentence showing their co-referentiality *(sāmānādhikaraṇya),* then we are entitled to say that such a sentence reveals that the product is unreal, as in the example: "this pot is clay".

जनितत्वमवादि न हि श्रुतिभिर्जनकेन सतास्य शरीरभृतः ।
मनआदिविकारविलक्षणतां प्रतियन्ति शरीरभृतस्तु ततः ॥६३॥

But the *śrutis* have not said that this embodied Self is produced by Brahman which is the Cause [of everything]. So [the wise] understand that the embodied Self cannot be compared to products such as the mind etc. (63)

comment

When we know that one thing is the material cause and that something is its product and when we come across a sentence expressing their co-referentiality, then we can understand that the sentence communicates that the product is unreal. But when a sentence expresses co-referentiality of two terms and one of the terms is not the product of the other, then the sentence does not reveal that one of the terms is unreal. No *śruti* says that the embodied Self is a product. So it is not unreal.

यदजीजनदम्बरपूर्वमिदं जगदक्षरमीक्षणविग्रहकम् ।
प्रविवेश तदेव जगत्स्वकृतं स च जीवसमाख्य इति श्रुतयः ॥६४॥

What the *śrutis* say is that the Immutable, having as Its form the knowledge [of what will be], produced this world beginning with space and entered into the very world He created. It is He [the supreme Self] who has the designation "individual soul" *[jīva].* (64)

comment

It is said in the *Chāndogya* Upaniṣad: "That Being visualised 'I will be many, I will be born'." (6.2.3). In the *Taittirīya* Upaniṣad it is said: "He desired, 'I will be many, I will be born.' He deliberated and having deliberated He emitted all this, whatever it is that exists. And having emitted it, He entered into it" (2.6.1).

The *śruti* does not say that the individual soul or *jīva* is an effect of Brahman; it says that the individual soul is Brahman. The matter of which the world consists, referred to by some Upaniṣads as "name-and-form" *(nāmarūpa),* has originated from Brahman. Brahman is metaphorically spoken of as "entering" into this matter as the individual soul or *jīva.* What is meant by "entry" is that although no form of matter is spatially separate from Brahman, Brahman is said to become manifest in the configurations of matter that are sufficiently subtle as to be capable of reflecting Awareness. The mind is a very subtle form of matter that is capable of reflecting Awareness. Brahman is the *jīva* under the conditioning factor of the individual mind, the senses and the physical body. Something that apparently conditions something else is called an *upādhi.* This important term was explained before, in the comment to verse seven. The body-sense-mind complex constitutes the *upādhi* and Brahman is called the "individual soul" in relation to a particular *upādhi.*

परमात्मविकारविभक्तमतिर्न भवत्यत एव शरीरभृतः ।
यत एव विकारविभिन्नमतिर्न भवत्यत एव मृषात्वमतिः ॥६५॥

अविभक्तविभक्त्यभिधानकृता परमात्मपदेन शरीरभृतः ।
न भवेदिह तत्त्वमसिप्रभृतौ लवणं जलमित्यभिधासु यथा ॥६६॥

Therefore there is no such idea that the embodied Self is separate on account of being a product of the supreme Self. Since there is no such idea of separation through being a product, you should not entertain the idea that in sentences such as *"tattvamasi"* the embodied Self is unreal just because the word denoting the supreme Self is used in grammatical apposition. It is similar to expressions such as "the water is salt". (65, 66)

comment

The last line of the previous verse, "It is He [the supreme Self] who has the designation "individual soul" *[jīva]"*, says that the individual soul is not a product of Brahman. Since the *jīva* is not a product, the apposition of *tat* and *tvam* in the sentence *"tattvamasi"* does not reveal that the *jīva* is unreal. In the case of the illustration "the water is salt", the salt is not a derivation of water, so the apposition of the terms does not give rise to the meaning that the salt is unreal.

The teacher now concludes his discussion of the objection raised in verse sixty.

परमात्मविकारनिराकरणं कृतमस्य शरीरभृतस्तु यतः ।
परमेश्वररूपविलक्षणता न मनागपि देहभृतोऽस्ति ततः ॥६७॥

Since the notion that the embodied Self is a product of the supreme Self has been refuted, there is therefore no difference at all between the embodied Self and the supreme Lord. (67)

The student asks:

ननु जीवसतोरणुमात्रमपि स्वगतं न विशेषणमस्ति यदा ।
वद तत्त्वमसीति तदा वचनं किमु वक्ति तथैष त इत्यपि च ॥ ६८॥

If there is not even a minute innate distinction between the individual soul and Brahman, then tell me, what do the sentences "you are That" and "This is your Self" say? (68)

comment

The student responds with a further objection. He says that if there is no difference at all between the individual soul and Brahman, what then is the purpose of the Vedānta teaching? If you are already Brahman, then would not the whole Vedānta teaching be redundant?

The teacher replies to this question.

स्वगतं यदि भेदकमिष्टमभूदणुमात्रमपीश्वरदेहभृतोः ।
अपनेतुमशक्यमदो वचनैरमुनास्य पृथक्त्वनिषेधपरैः ॥६९॥

If even a minute innate distinction is accepted between the Lord and the embodied Self, the sentences [such as *tattvamasi]*, which aim to negate the separation of the embodied Self with the Lord, would be unable to remove that distinction. (69)

The teacher further explains this point.

इह यस्य च यो गुण आत्मगतः स्वत एव न जातु भवेत्परतः ।
वचनेन न तस्य निराकरणं क्रियते स गुणः सहजस्तु यतः ॥७०॥

When a thing has an inherent attribute, the attribute would never be contingent upon something else. A sentence does not negate that attribute, because it is intrinsic. (70)

comment

The student asked what is the point of the statement *"tattvamasi"* if we are already Brahman. The teaching therefore seems to be useless. The teacher replies by saying that if the Self and Brahman were really different, the sentence *tattvamasi* would be unable to alter that fact. We can see that if a substance has an inherent quality, like sugar is naturally sweet, then merely saying that sugar is bitter is not going to remove the sweetness which is inherent to sugar. Likewise, if there is a real difference between the Self and Brahman, then a mere statement to the contrary cannot remove that difference.

वचनं त्ववबोधकमेव यतस्तत एव न वस्तुविपर्ययकृत् ।
न हि वस्त्वपि शब्दवशात्प्रकृतिं प्रजहात्यनवस्थितिदोषभयात् ॥७१॥

Because the sentence is just informative, it does not cause a thing to alter its nature. Nor does the thing itself abandon its own nature on account of the power of the words, for fear of the defect that it would not continue to exist. (71)

comment

The sentence *"tattvamasi"* merely communicates knowledge. In doing so, the sentence functions as a *pramāṇa,* a means of knowledge. The means of knowledge that we use in everyday activities, such as perception and inference, are meant to reveal their respective objects. Perceptual knowledge arises from our senses and each of the senses is only meant to reveal what already exists, as that thing really is. The sense of sight is meant to reveal the tree nearby and it is meant to reveal the tree as a tree, not as something else. A *pramāṇa,* therefore, is meant to accurately reveal what exists. According to Vedānta, the sentence *tattvamasi* is a *pramāṇa* which reveals to us an unknown fact, namely that we are essentially Brahman. The sentence, like any *pramāṇa,* is just meant to reveal its object. It cannot cause a thing to alter its nature. So if there is a difference between the Self and Brahman, the sentence cannot alter that fact.

Nor does a thing change itself so as to conform to the sentence. If a thing relinquished its inherent quality, such as sugar gave up its sweetness so as to agree with the statement that sugar is bitter, then the thing would have abandoned its inherent nature and that would result in its destruction.

How then does the sentence *tattvamasi* communicate? The teacher says:

यत एवमतो विषयस्य गुणं विषयेण सहात्मनि मूढधिया ।
अधिरोपितमप्स्विव भूमिगुणं प्रतिषेधति तत्त्वमसीति वचः ॥७२॥

Since that is so, therefore, the sentence *"tattvamasi"* negates the attribute of the object, along with the object itself, which an ignorant person has superimposed upon the Self. It is analogous to the way a sentence negates the attribute of earth that has been superimposed in water. (72)

comment

If the difference between the Self and Brahman is real, then no sentence can alter that fact. If, however, the difference is not real, but is superimposed because of the identification with limiting adjuncts *(aupādhikabheda),* then the sentence can reveal the inherent identity once the difference brought about by the limiting adjuncts has been negated. The sentence *"tattvamasi"* reveals a positive truth, namely that the essence of any individual is identical to the Absolute Being. The sentence reveals this truth when it negates the limiting adjuncts of the body-sense-mind complex, and their attributes, which a person ordinarily understands to be himself or herself. Thus the sentence reveals a positive truth through negating superimposition.

The teacher says the sentence *"tattvamasi"* is akin to a statement like "earth has the attribute of smell". According to the teaching of the five elements, the element earth has the special attribute of smell. Water is considered to be naturally without smell. So if we find water that smells, we know that the water has been contaminated with the products of earth. The statement like "earth has the attribute of smell" serves to negate the smell as something that has been superimposed in water. Similarly, the sentence *"tattvamasi"* reveals the real nature of the Self through the negation of superimposed difference which belongs to the *upādhi* of the body-mind complex.

The teacher now returns to the principal topic and continues the refutation begun in verse fifty-five.

अत एव न दृष्टिविधानपरं गुणवादपरं च न तद्वचनम् ।
स्तुतिवाद्यपि नैतदुपास्यतया विधिरत्र न देहभृतोऽस्ति यतः ॥७३॥

Therefore the sentence *[tattvamasi]* is not meant to prescribe a conceptual meditation, because there is no injunction here that the embodied Self ought to be conceptually meditated upon [as Brahman]. Nor is that sentence intended as a metaphor, nor is it even a type of praise. (73)

comment

In verses forty-nine to fifty-two the student put forward four possible ways of interpreting a statement such as *"tattvamasi"*. The answer to the first of these possibilities was begun in verse fifty-five to fifty-nine. The topic is again taken up here. A conceptual meditation *(upāsanā)* is presented as something to be performed. It is generally in the form of an injunction, such as "one should meditate upon the mind as Brahman" etc. In the case of the sentence *"tattvamasi"*, however, there is no injunction to do anything. The verse *"asi"* just reveals that you *are* Brahman. Therefore the sentence *"tattvamasi"* is an entirely different type of statement from a statement having to do with an *upāsanā*. Nor is the sentence a metaphor etc. because when it is shown that the sentence can be understood in its primary sense, it is unwarranted to search for a figurative meaning.

The teacher now takes up the fourth possibility.

सत एव हि नाम जगत्प्रकृतेरुपधानवशादिह जीव इति ।

अत एव न जीवसतत्त्वकतां प्रकृतस्य सतः प्रतिपादयति ॥७४॥

Brahman itself, the material cause of the world, is called the "individual soul" *(jīva)* on account of limiting adjuncts. Since that is so, [the sentence *"tattvamasi"]* does not convey the knowledge that Brahman, who is the subject-matter of the Upaniṣad sentences, has actually acquired the nature of the individual soul. (74)

comment

In verse fifty-two the student said: "Or else, the sentence might be saying that Brahman has actually acquired the nature of an individual soul who is expressed in the *śruti* by the word 'you'." Instead of saying "you are That", the sentence could be saying "That is you", i.e. Brahman has become the *saṁsārijīva.* The teacher takes up this point and says that what we call an "individual self", or *jīva,* is Brahman in association with the limiting adjuncts *(upādhi)* of the body-sense-mind complex. All differences pertain only to the *upādhi,* not to the essential Being which is Brahman itself. Since there is no such entity as a *jīva* existing in its own right, independently from an *upādhi,* the sentence does not say that Brahman has become a *jīva,* what it says is that the essential nature of the *aupādhikajīva* is Brahman.

The teacher continues his refutation of this point.

यदि जीवसतत्त्वकतां गमयेदणिमादिगुणस्य जगत्प्रकृतेः ।
अणिमादिगुणोक्तिरतोऽस्य मृषा यदि वास्य शरीरभृदात्मकता ॥७५॥

If [the sentence *"tattvamasi"]* makes known that Brahman, who has the quality of being the subtle essence etc. [of everything], and who is the material cause of the world, has actually acquired the nature of an individual soul, then the statement that Brahman has the quality of being the subtle essence etc. must be false. Or, if Brahman does have the quality of being the subtle essence etc., then [the conjecture] that Brahman has acquired the nature of the embodied Self must be false. (75)

comment

The full *Chāndogya* text in which the sentence *"tattvamasi"* occurs is as follows: "That which is this subtle essence, everything has this essence as its Self. That is real. That is the Self. You are That, Śvetaketu!" (6.8.7 ff.). If Brahman, characterised as the "subtle essence" of everything, has become the individual soul, then Brahman cannot be the subtle essence of everything because Brahman has become a finite entity, namely the embodied Self who is subject to pleasure, pain, desire, anger, anxiety etc. But if Brahman is the subtle essence of everything, then Brahman cannot have become the individual soul.

There is a further reason why the opposite meaning of the sentence *"tattvamasi"* should not be accepted.

न च संसृतिहेतुनिराकरणं कृतमस्य शरीरभृतोऽभिमतम् ।
परमेश्वरमात्मतया ब्रुवता वचनेन च तत्त्वमसीत्यमुना ॥७६॥

And the removal of the cause of transmigratory existence, which is something desirable to the embodied Self, would not be accomplished by the sentence *"tattvamasi"* when it says that the supreme Lord is the [individual] self. (76)

In the next five verses the teacher gives a further reason, based upon the grammatical procedure of connecting the words in the sentence.

त्वमसीति-पदद्वयमेति युजां तदिति ध्वनिना सह तत्त्वमिति ।
क्रियया सह नामपदं समियान्निरपेक्षमुपैत्यनया हि युजाम् ॥७७॥

The two words "you" *[tvam]* and "are" *[asi]* are connected with the word "That" *[tad]:* "you are That". The word ["That"] has to be connected to the verb, for when it is connected with the verb [the sentence] does not leave any expectancy. (77)

comment

How do we understand the sentence *"tattvamasi"?* In this sentence *"tattvamasi"* we firstly connect the two words *"tvam"* ["you"] and *"asi"* ["are"], for it is most natural to firstly connect the subject and the verb. The statement that "you are" would create an expectancy for predication. The hearer would understand "I am...?" and then wait for the predicate to reveal what he or she is. The word *"tat"* ["that"] must then be connected to the verb, for it is only when the predicate is connected to the verb that the expectation of the hearer is removed. Hence the natural way of understanding the sentence is "you are That". The teacher further explains this verse in the following verses.

न हि नामसहस्रमपि क्रियया रहितं किमपि प्रतिपादयति ।
प्रतिपादकमेषु लिङादि भवेद्विहितादिमतेर्जनकं हि यतः ॥७८॥

Even a thousand words do not convey any meaning if they are without a verb. Among these [words in a sentence], it is the verbal forms that can convey the meaning, because they produce the understanding that something has to be done [or not done] etc. (78)

comment

The verb is the most important element in the sentence. A group of words do not convey a coherent meaning if they are not connected to a verb. When the words are connected to the verb, the verb conveys the sentence meaning by connecting the subject to some action or state, eg. "Devadatta, you should bring the cow."; "Yajñadatta, you should not touch the cow."; "Somadatta, you know where the rope is kept." Etc.

भगवानपि मध्यममेव यतो विनियच्छति युष्मदि नित्यमतः ।
प्रथमं त्वमसीति पदे समितश्चरमं त्वसिना समियात्तदिति ॥७९॥

Moreover the revered Pāṇini has made the invariable rule that only the verb in the second person is to be used with the second person pronoun, therefore the two words *"tvam"* and *"asi"* connect first and then the word *"tad"* should join with *"asi"*. (79)

comment

In verse seventy-seven it was said that the two words *"tvam"* and *"asi"* are linked together first and then these two words connect with the word *"tad"*. In this verse the teacher cites Pāṇini as the authority as to why *"tvam"* and *"asi"* must be connected first. There is a Pāṇini *sūtra* (1.4.105) which says that the verb in the second person is to be used when the second person pronoun [you] is expressed or understood. Therefore the second person pronoun *"tvam"* and the second person singular *"asi"* are grammatically related, and so they must be connected first. The word *"tad"* has therefore to be connected to the verb *"asi"* subsequently. So the sentence must be understood as "you are That".

पुरुषोऽभिहितस्त्वमसीति यदा किमसानि वदेति तदाभिमुखः ।
श्रवणाय भवेदणिमादिगुणं सदिति प्रकृतं तदसीति वदेत् ॥८०॥

When the person is told "you are" *(tvam asi)*, there would be a readiness to hear [with the expectation]: "what can I be? Tell me!" The [teacher] would say, referring to Brahman who is the subject matter of the discussion and who has the quality of being the subtle essence [of everything]: "you are That" *(tad asi)*. (80)

comment

Verse seventy-seven also mentioned the idea of expectancy. Once the two words *"tvam"* and *"asi"* are connected, the meaning is "you are" and there arises the natural expectancy on the part of the hearer: "what am I?" The word *"tad"* - which refers to the pure Being which is the context of the whole discussion - is then predicated and the predicate removes the listener's expectancy. Thus the correct manner of understanding the sentence is "you are That Being".

The teacher now concludes the discussion about whether the sentence can have the opposite meaning.

त्वमिति ध्वनिनाभिहितस्य यतस्तदिति श्रुतिवाच्यसदात्मकताम् ।
अवदद्वचनं तत एव सतो न हि जीवसतत्त्वकतां वदति ॥८१॥

Since the sentence has stated that the one who is addressed by the word "you" is identical to Brahman which is expressed in the *śruti* by the word "That", the sentence therefore does not say that Brahman has become the individual soul. (81)

The teacher now takes up the objection that was put forward in verse fifty-three.

विषयाभिमुखानि शरीरभृतः स्वरसेन सदा करणानि यतः ।
स्वकमेष न रूपमवैति ततः प्रतिबोध्यत एव ततो वचनैः ॥८२॥

Because the sense-organs of the embodied Self are, of their own accord, always oriented toward sense-objects, that is why he does not understand his own inherent nature. And that is why it is only revealed by the *śruti* statements. (82)

comment

An objection was raised in verse fifty-three that if the embodied Self is always Brahman, then why is the Self not aware of this fact? The teacher answers that the reason why we fail to recognise our own inherent nature is that our sense-organs, i.e. the sense of seeing, hearing, smelling, tasting and touching, are naturally object-oriented. We are always engrossed in the experience of one thing or another and we do not so much as reflect on who is the Experiencer.

Even if we do reflect on the Experiencer, how can we know the nature of the Experiencer since the Experiencer is not a sense-object?

Perhaps if we distinguish the Self from the non-Self, by a process of discriminative reasoning based on the distinction between subject and object, we will discover the real nature of the Self? But even this reasoning is not sufficient on its own, for we will be left with the radical dualism of a knower over against the known, as in Sāṅkhya. The Vedānta says that the real nature of the Self is not revealed by mere discrimination, though that is an important preparatory step, but it is revealed by the Upaniṣads which, in teaching the real nature of the Self, remove ignorance and along with that the sense of finitude.

The teacher cites some statements from the *śruti* and *smṛti* which tell that the senses are externally-orientated and do not reveal the inner-Self.

वचनं च पराञ्चिपुरःसरकं बहु वैदिकमत्र तथा स्मरणम् ।
विषयेषु च नावमिवाम्भसि यन्मनसेन्द्रियरश्मिविनिग्रहवत् ॥८३॥

There are many Vedic statements which refer to this, such as the one beginning with: "external". Similarly, there are statements in the tradition such as: "[the mind, acting in compliance with the senses moving] among the sense-objects, [carries off a person's wisdom, like the wind] carries away a boat at sea". ["Restraining the senses] just by the mind". "Restraining the reins of the senses". (83)

comment

In the Upaniṣads, and in *smṛti* texts such as the *Bhagavadgītā,* there are many statements which tell that the senses are a natural obstruction to understanding the nature of the Self. The first quotation, from the *Kaṭha* Upaniṣad, says: "The self-existent Lord made the external senses worthless, therefore one sees the outer things and not the inner-Self" (2.1.). In the *Bhagavadgītā* there is the statement: "The mind, acting in compliance with the senses moving [among the sense-objects], carries off a person's wisdom, like the wind carries away a boat at sea" (2.67.). Also, "Restraining all of the senses just by the mind, one should slowly quieten [the mind] through the intellect which is imbued with resolve, and making the mind rest in the Self, one should not think about anything"

(6. 24-25.). In another *smṛti* text there is the statement: "When the person restrains the organs of knowledge, which are 'the reins', along with the mind, then the Self shines, just like a light shining within a jar".

इयता हि न देहभृतोऽस्ति भिदा परमात्मदृशेरिति वाच्यमिदम्।
स्थितिकाल इहापि च सृष्टिमुखे सदनन्यतया श्रुत एष यतः ॥८४॥

You should not say that just because of this [i.e. from the above quotations] the embodied Self is different from the Seeing which is the Supreme Self. Because the embodied Self is revealed by the *śruti* to be non-different from Brahman at the time of the origination of the world, as well as now while the world exists. (84)

comment

The student should not think that the *śruti* says there is difference between the individual self and Brahman just because the above quotations did not speak of identity, for the purport of the *śruti* is only in the identity of the Self as Brahman.

The teacher concludes his discussion of this objection with the following verse.

द्वयमप्यविरोधि शरीरभृतो वचनीयमिदं रघुनन्दनवत्।
उपदेशमपेक्ष्य सदात्ममतिः परमात्मसतत्त्वकता च सदा ॥८५॥

It has to be said that with regard to the embodied Self even both these do not present a contradiction, namely that the knowledge of oneself as Brahman is a matter requiring instruction, and the fact that one is always identical to the supreme Self. It is analogous to the situation of Śrī Rāma. (85)

comment

We are always Brahman, through we are not aware of the fact. Our sense-organs reveal only sense-objects and they are not competent to reveal what is not a sense-object, namely the Self. Inference depends upon perception and so it too is not competent to reveal the Self who is not an object. And the knowledge derived from inference would, in any case, be only an indirect knowledge. The Upaniṣads are the means of knowledge *(pramāṇa)* to reveal the true nature of the inner-Self. The Upaniṣads should be taught by a teacher who knows how to use the Upaniṣad words to point out the real nature of the Self. Thus there is the requirement of the scripture, i.e the *śāstra,* and the teacher, i.e. the *ācārya.* The *ācārya,* furthermore, ought to know the traditional method of teaching *(saṁpradāyavit).* There is also the requirement that the student be ready to receive the teaching.

According to Vedānta, the words of the *śruti* are the means of knowledge to reveal that the Self is Brahman. If a person is already Brahman, but does not know this, then instruction is necessary to enlighten a person as to their real nature. The teacher gives the illustration of Lord Rāma. Rāma was the incarnation of Viṣṇu. The purpose of this incarnation was to destroy the demon Rāvaṇa. Rāma, however, did not know that he was the incarnation of Lord Viṣṇu; he thought he was an ordinary man, the son of King Daśaratha. After Rāma had killed the demon Rāvaṇa, the god Brahmā revealed to Rāma that he was really Viṣṇu. Though Rāma was already Viṣṇu, the knowledge of the fact required instruction. Similarly, though we are already Brahman, on account of ignorance of the fact we require instruction.

According to the maxim of "the lion's glance" *(siṁhāvalokananyāya),* i.e. how a lion, while travelling across country, casts an occasional backward glance over the territory he has passed, the teacher again takes up to the topic of *upāsanā.*

सदुपासनमस्य विधेयतया वचनस्य मम प्रतिभाति यतः ।
अत एव न जीवसदात्मकतां प्रतिबोधयतीत्यवदत्तदसत् ॥८६॥

[The student had] said: "since this sentence *[tattvamasi]* seems to me to enjoin a conceptual meditation on Brahman, it does not therefore reveal that the individual soul is Brahman". That is not true. (86)

comment

The student had raised a series of objections in verses forty-nine to fifty-four. The most serious of the objections was that the sentence *"tattvamasi"* is meant only as a type of conceptual meditation *(upāsanā)*. While the teacher was dealing with this objection the student raised a further question, at verse sixty, and again at verse sixty-eight. After answering these two questions the teacher returned to discuss the remaining objections that the student had stated in verses forty-nine to fifty-four. Now the teacher returns to the topic of *upāsanā* and discusses it elaborately from verse eighty-six to verse one hundred and seven. In the present verse he refers to what the student had said back in verse forty-nine.

सदुपास्व इति श्रुतिरत्र न ते तदसि त्वमिति श्रुतिरेवमियम् ।
यत एवमतो न विधित्सितता सदुपासनकर्मण इत्यमृषा ॥८७॥

Here [in the case of the sentence *tattvamasi]*, the *śruti* does not say to you: "you must conceptually meditate upon Brahman". The *śruti* sentence says: "you are That". Since this is so, we are therefore correct when we say that the action of conceptual meditation on Brahman is not intended to be enjoined. (87)

यदि तस्य कुतश्चिदिहानयनं क्रियते तदनर्थकमेव भवेत् ।
पुरुषेण कृतस्य यतः श्रुतिता न भवेदिति वेदविदां स्मरणम् ॥८८॥

If [you think that] an injunctive word is supplied here from some other sentence, that injunction would have no effect. Because the traditional understanding of those who know the Veda is that whatever is created by a person cannot be *śruti.* (88)

comment

It is evident that the sentence *"tattvamasi"* contains no injunction of any kind. The hearer is not told to do anything. Suppose we take an injunction from some other passage in the *śruti* and apply it here to the sentence *tattvamasi.* The teacher says it would be wrong to suggest such a procedure. Since the *śruti* is an independent means of knowledge *(svataḥ pramāṇa),* we must not tamper with the *śruti,* but take the *śruti* as it is.

The teacher says, with a touch of sarcasm:

किमरे पुरुषं प्रतिबोधयितुं स्वकमर्थमशक्तमिदं वचनम् ।
यदतोऽन्यत आनयनं क्रियते भवता श्रवणेन विनापि विधेः ॥८९॥

Oh! Is this sentence *[tattvamasi]* so incapable of revealing its meaning to a person that even without hearing an injunction you would bring it from somewhere else? (89)

He points out the consequence of introducing an injunction.

श्रुतहानिरिहाश्रुतक्लृप्तिरपि श्रुतिवित्समयो न भवेत्तु यतः ।
श्रुतिभक्तिमता श्रुतिवक्त्रगतं ग्रहणीयमतो न तु बुद्धिवशात् ॥९०॥

But here [in the case where an injunctive word is supplied from somewhere else], because there would be the loss of what is directly heard as well as the supposition of what is not directly heard, there would be no agreement among those who know the *śruti.* Therefore a person who has devotion to the *śruti* should take what comes from the mouth of the *śruti* rather than rely upon his own conjecture. (90)

comment

If an injunction is supplied from somewhere else the result would be the "loss of what is directly heard" *(śrutahāni)* and the "supposition of what is not directly heard" *(aśrutakalpanā)*, because the meaning of the sentence as it is heard would be given up and a meaning other than what is heard would be conjectured. The result would be that no one would be able to agree about the meaning of a sentence. Therefore we must take the *śruti* as it is.

One should not think that the *śruti* sentence, such as *tattvamasi*, is of no purpose because it does not enjoin the hearer to undertake some kind of action.

पुरुषस्य शरीरगतात्ममतिं मृतिसंभवहेतुमनर्थकरीम् ।
अपनीय सदात्ममतिं दधती महते पुरुषस्य हिताय भवेत् ॥९१॥

[The *śruti]*, upon removing the idea that the Self is the body - an idea which lies at the source of a person's suffering and is the cause of repeated birth and death - conveys the understanding that the Self is Brahman, so it would prove of immense benefit to a person. (91)

comment

Among the traditionally accepted goals of a human life *(puruṣārtha)*, i.e. right conduct *(dharma)*, material security *(artha)*, the satisfaction of desires *(kāma)*, and liberation *(mokṣa)*, Vedānta is concerned with *mokṣa*. The first three goals neither presuppose the knowledge of reality, nor do they directly produce the knowledge of reality. *Dharma*, *artha* and *kāma* function within the sphere of everyday life *(vyavahāra)* and presuppose the erroneous superimposition *(adhyāsa)* between the Self and the physical body. The Vedānta knowledge, stemming from the Upaniṣad words, removes superimposition and reveals the real nature of the Self and the world. This knowledge, through the negation of superimposition, and by pointing out the true nature of the Self, shows that sadness is an error of thought. The Vedānta is therefore of supreme benefit and it is not correct to say that it has no benefit because it deals with Being and not with doing.

विनिवर्तत एव शरीरगता विपरीतमतिः पुरुषस्य तदा ।
वचनेन तु तत्त्वमसीति यदा प्रतिबोध्यत एष त इत्यपि च ॥९२॥

When [the person] is awakened through the statement "you are That" and "This is your Self", at that very time the person's erroneous idea about [the Self being just] the body comes to an end. (92)

comment

Not only do the Vedānta sentences have value, but they can directly produce the liberating understanding provided the hearer is ready to receive what is conveyed through the medium of the words. If the hearer is thoroughly ready *(uttamādhikārin),* then the liberating meaning of the sentence *"tattvamasi"* can be comprehended even at the very time of hearing the sentence. Hearing the teaching can immediately awaken such a person to the direct understanding of reality and the erroneous idea of identity with the physical body will then cease.

The teacher now shows the unacceptable consequences of maintaining that *"tattvamasi"* teaches an *upāsanā.*

यदि नापनयेच्छ्रुतिरात्ममतिं पुरुषस्य शरीरगतामनृताम् ।
तदहंमतिहेतुककर्मगतिं सुखदुःखफलामवशोऽनुभवेत् ॥९३॥

If the *śruti* could not remove the person's erroneous notion that the Self is the body, then the person would have no alternative but to experience the course of the consequences of past deeds *(karma),* which are themselves the result of the ego-notion. And that course will result in pleasure and pain. (93)

Furthermore:

यदि तत्त्वमसीति वदेद्वचनं सदुपासनकर्म न तत्त्वमिति ।
पुरुषस्य फलं सदुपासनतो विमृशामि भविष्यति कीदृगिति ॥९४॥

If the sentence *"tattvamasi"* speaks of an action consisting of the conceptual meditation on Brahman, and it does not say "you are That", then I wonder what sort of result a person will get from this type of a meditation on Brahman? (94)

comment

The teacher implies that nothing will come of it. The reason is given in the next verse.

पुरुषस्य तु मर्त्यगुणस्य भवेत्सदुपासनया न सदात्मकता ।
न कथञ्चिदपि प्रजहाति यतः प्रकृतिं सहजामिह कश्चिदपि ॥९५॥

A person whose attribute is mortality could not become Brahman through a conceptual meditation upon Brahman, for there is no way that someone can abandon their intrinsic nature. (95)

comment

If the embodied Self is intrinsically other than Brahman, then the Self can never become Brahman. Because in order to do so the Self would have to give up its own nature and that would result in its destruction. The teacher here echoes the statement of Gauḍapāda: "The immortal does not become mortal, nor does the mortal become immortal. In no circumstances will a thing change its intrinsic nature." (3.21).

The teacher then says that if the embodied Self does become Brahman through *upāsanā*, then the Self would have to give up its own nature.

यदि देहभृदेष सदात्मकतां प्रगमिष्यति वै सदुपासनया ।
न जहास्यति रूपमसौ हि निजं यत ऐक्यमतिर्न भवत्युभयोः ॥९६॥

If this embodied Self does become Brahman through a conceptual meditation upon Brahman, will the Self not abandon its own nature? Because there can be no idea of oneness between both [as long as they are intrinsically distinct in nature]. (96)

comment

The teacher argued in verse ninety-five that if the embodied Self is intrinsically different from Brahman there is no way that the Self can become Brahman through a process of *upāsanā*, because one thing cannot become another thing. In verse ninety-six he says that if the embodied Self, though different from Brahman, does somehow become Brahman through *upāsanā*, then the Self would have to give up its own nature. To do so would amount to its destruction.

The student raises an objection.

रसविद्धमयः प्रकृतिं सहजां प्रविहाय यथा कनकत्वमियात् ।
पुरुषोऽपि तथा सदुपासनया प्रतिपत्स्यत एव सदात्मकताम् ॥९७॥

Just as iron, when mixed with mercury, gives up its own nature and transmutes into gold, so too a person will definitely attain the nature of Brahman though the conceptual meditation upon Brahman. (97)

comment

The student says that it is possible that something can give up its own nature and change into something else without being destroyed in the process. For example, when iron is mixed with mercury, the substance which was known as iron does not cease to exist, but what happens is that the substance ceases to be iron and turns into gold. So likewise it is possible for the individual soul, through *upāsanā*, to give up its own mortal nature and to become Brahman without undergoing destruction.

The teacher replies that the illustration itself is wrong.

अयसोऽवयवानभिभूय रसः स्थितवाननलानुगृहीतिमनु ।
कनकत्वमतिं जनयत्ययसि प्रतिपन्नमयो न तु काञ्चनताम् ॥९८॥

The heated mercury, plating the iron, conceals the constituents of iron and produces the idea that the iron has become gold. But in fact the iron has not become gold. (98)

उदकावयवानभिभूय पयो रजतावयवांश्च यथा कनकम् ।
विपरीतमतिं जनयत्युदके रजते च तथायसि हेममतिम् ॥९९॥

Just as milk conceals the constituents of water and produces the opposite idea about the water [namely that it is milk] and just as gold conceals the constituents of silver and produces the opposite idea about the silver [that it is gold], in the same way [the mercury] produces the idea that iron has become gold. (99)

रसवीर्यविपाकविनाशमनु प्रविनश्यति काञ्चनताप्ययसः ।
कृतकं हि न नित्यमिति प्रगतं समवेतमवश्यमपैति यतः ॥१००॥

Moreover the golden appearance of the iron is lost once the change brought about by the potency of the mercury comes to an end. For things that come together inevitably get separated, on the principle that "whatever is created is not permanent". (100)

The teacher raises another possibility and refutes it:

अमृतत्वमसत्पुरुषस्य यदि क्रियते सदुपासनया यजिवत् ।
यजिकार्यवदन्तवदेव भवेत्कृतकस्य यतो विदिताध्रुवता ॥१०१॥

Suppose a person is not immortal, but immortality is created by the action of the conceptual meditation upon Brahman, like how something is produced by performing a sacrificial rite. Then immortality would definitely come to an end, in the same way as whatever is produced by the rite comes to an end. For it is a known fact that whatever is created is impermanent. (101)

comment

It could be argued that a mortal person can gain a permanent place in heaven though the performance of an impermanent action, namely the Vedic rite. In the same way, why could not the mortal person become deathless through the performance of the conceptual meditation upon Brahman? The teacher says it is not possible that something permanent can be produced through an action. According to the Chāndogya *śruti,* the result of an action is not permanent, even in the case of heaven: "Just as here, the world won by action perishes, so too there, the world won by virtuous deeds perishes." (8.1.6). Therefore even the place in heaven is not permanent, because it is brought about through action. Deathlessness cannot be brought into being by performing some kind of action, whether it is a Vedic ritual, or the practice of *upāsanā.* The *śruti,* and our own observation of things in the world, tell us that something that is brought into being cannot be permanent.

पुरुषस्य सतश्च विधर्मकयोः सदुपासनया न भवेत्समितिः ।
यदि संगतिरिष्यत एव तयोरवियुक्ततया न चिरं वसतः ॥१०२॥

No union can take place between the person and Brahman through the conceptual meditation upon Brahman, as both have opposing attributes.

If you think that their union does occur, then they would not remain for long without separation. (102)

comment

Suppose it is said that the individual soul does not become Brahman but becomes united with Brahman through *upāsanā.* In this way the individual soul will not have to undergo a change of nature and can avoid the consequence of destruction since the individual soul has not actually become Brahman. The teacher says it is not possible to unite two things that have opposite natures. We cannot unite the mortal individual self and the deathless Brahman because they have opposing natures. But if somehow they do become united, then the teacher says they will not remain united for long because whenever there is conjunction there will be disjunction. There is a well known saying found, for example, in the *Rāmāyaṇa,* which says: "all unions end in separation" *(saṁyogā viprayogāntāḥ)* (2.98.16).

फलमीदृगिदं सदुपासनतः पुरुषस्य भविष्यति नान्यदतः ।
न च तन्निरवद्यतयाभिमतं विदुषां बहुदोषसमीक्षणतः ॥१०३॥

This is the type of result that a person will get from the conceptual meditation upon Brahman. There can be no other result than this. And learned people do not look upon that result as something unobjectionable, for it is found to have so many defects. (103)

comment

If it is said that the mortal individual soul can become the immortal Brahman through a process of *upāsanā,* then the individual soul would have to give up its essential nature and that would amount to its destruction. Furthermore, if the mortal individual could become immortal as a result of *upāsanā,* that new condition would be impermanent because it has been brought into being. However, if it is said that the individual soul does not actually become Brahman but becomes united with Brahman because of *upāsanā,* even that is not possible, because things having opposing qualities cannot be united. And even if they could be united they would again become separate, since things which are joined together will become separated. So *upāsanā* has only such results as stated above. It cannot produce a permanent result because it is an action and the product of an action is impermanent. Therefore the individual soul is already Brahman, or it is not Brahman. If the individual soul is Brahman, and the soul does not understand that it is Brahman, then the *śruti* is meant to reveal this truth to the individual soul. If the individual soul is not Brahman, there is no way that it can become Brahman.

What then does the sentence do? The teacher says:

सदुपासनकर्मविधानपरं न भवेदत एव हि तद्वचनम् ।
अहमस्मि शरीरमिदं च ममेत्यविवेकमतिं विनिवर्तयति ॥१०४॥

Therefore the sentence *[tattvamasi]* cannot be intended to enjoin an action consisting of the conceptual meditation upon Brahman. The sentence removes the notions "I am this body", "this body is mine", which arise out of a lack of discrimination. (104)

comment

The sentence *tattvamasi* reveals the essential nature of the person and when the knowledge arises, the false notions cease. The false notions are based upon the superimposition *(adhyāsa)* of the body and the Self, such as: "I am a man", "I am a woman", "I am a Brāhmaṇa", "I am a householder", "I am a renouncer" etc. These ideas are based upon the physical body and its particular status. The sentence also removes the idea of "mine", namely the superimposition that the attributes of the body are the attributes of the Self. The sentence reveals the real nature of the Self and in doing so it removes the wrong notions that are superimposed on the Self out of ignorance.

सकलोपनिषत्सु शरीरभृतः परमात्मपदैकविभक्तितया ।

उपदेशवचांस्यनयैव दिशा गमयेन्मतिमानभियुक्ततया ॥१०५॥

Since we find that in all the Upaniṣads the embodied Self is in grammatical apposition with a word denoting the supreme Self, an intelligent person should diligently construe the statements which teach [the true nature of the Self] in this same way [i.e. as revealing oneness through negating superimposition, but not as teaching *upāsanā* or as having a metaphorical meaning etc.]. (105)

comment

In verse fifty-four the student had said that the sentence *"tattvamasi"* should be interpreted as presenting a type of *upāsanā,* or as having some other meaning such as a metaphor, or as a way of praising the individual, or even as teaching the opposite meaning. And he said that any other similar statement in the *śruti* should be interpreted in one of these ways, but not as teaching that the real nature of the individual soul is Brahman. The teacher refers to that statement when he says that any *śruti* text that instructs about the nature of the Self should be interpreted only as teaching that the Self is Brahman and thereby removing ignorance and superimposition. The reason why a text should only be interpreted in this way is that it invariably presents the embodied Self as co-referential with Brahman, as is the case in the statement: "you are That". In all the Upaniṣads we will find co-referentiality *(sāmānādhikaraṇya)* between the Self and a word referring to Brahman. Since there is co-referentiality, we are not entitled to interpret the *śruti* sentence as having some other meaning, such as prescribing an *upāsanā*, or as having only a metaphorical sense.

द्रविडोऽपि च तत्त्वमसीति वचो विनिवर्तकमेव निरूपितवान् ।
शबरेण विवर्धितराजशिशोर्निजजन्मविदुक्तिनिदर्शनतः ॥१०६॥

Draviḍa too has determined that the sentence *"tattvamasi"* only removes [false notions]. For he has cited the illustration of Śabara, who raised the child of a king, and knowing the child's birthright, told him [that he was a prince]. (106)

comment

Draviḍācārya was a Vedāntin before the time of Śaṅkara. He composed a commentary *(bhāṣya)* upon a brief exposition of the *Chāndogya* Upaniṣad by an earlier Vedāntin named Brahmanandī. Only fragments of these works are now available. Draviḍācārya refers to a story in the course of his explanation of the *mahāvākya "tattvamasi"*. He says that a prince was brought up by a hunter named Śabara. The boy naturally thought that he too was a hunter by birth. Śabara, however, knew the truth of the situation and revealed to the boy that he was not a hunter but a prince. When the boy understood this, he gave up his previous idea that he belonged by birth to a hunter's family. Similarly, the statement *"tattvamasi"* removes the wrong notions about the Self, it does not produce something that does not already exist.

यत एवमतः स्वशरीरगतामहमित्यविवेकमतिं सुदृढाम् ।
प्रविहाय यदक्षरमद्वयकं त्वमवेहि तदक्षरमात्मतया ॥१०७॥

Since this is so, therefore, giving up the firmly entrenched notion of "I" in one's physical body, a notion that arises from a lack of discrimination, you must know that the Imperishable, which is without duality, is the Self. (107)

comment

The teacher here concludes the topic as to whether the sentence *"tattvamasi"* describes an *upāsanā*, or reveals that the Self is Brahman. He has shown that it does not teach an *upāsanā*, nor any of the other meanings the student had suggested. In this verse the teacher addresses the pupil. He says that it has been shown that the sentence reveals the essential identity between the individual soul and Brahman and removes the error of superimposition. So the student should grasp the meaning of the sentence for himself: he should relinquish the erroneous identification of the Self with the body and its attributes and he should understand that the essential Self is none other than Brahman which is non-dual.

The teacher now instructs the student about the nature of Brahman *(tat)* and about the nature of the Self *(tvam)* to facilitate the student in coming to this understanding. In the following two verses he indicates the nature of Brahman.

न मनो न मतिः करणानि च नो न रजो न तमो न च सत्त्वमपि ।
न मही न जलं न च वह्निरपि श्वसनो न नभश्च पदं परमम् ॥१०८॥

अमनस्कमधीकमनिन्द्रियकं विरजस्कमसत्त्वतमस्कमपि ।
अमहीजलवह्न्यनिलाम्बरकं परमक्षरमात्मतयाश्रय भोः ॥१०९॥

The supreme Reality is not the mind, not the intellect and not the senses. It is not activity *(rajas)*, not dullness *(tamas)*, nor even tranquillity *(sattva)*. It is not earth, not water, nor even fire, neither is it air nor space. (108)

The supreme Imperishable has no mind, no intellect and no senses. It has no activity, nor even does it have tranquillity or dullness. It possesses neither earth, water, fire, air nor space. That supreme Imperishable, O student, you must come to accept as the Self! (109)

comment

In these two verses, the teacher indicates the meaning of the word *tat* through the negation of all objects of Awareness. All objective things are "name-and-form" *(nāmarūpa)*. Verse one hundred and eight points out that Brahman is not the mind, not the intellect etc. The next verse shows that Brahman is free from any inherent connection to the mind etc.

In the following three verses the teacher discusses the characteristics of the states of waking, dream and dreamless sleep, in order to reveal the real nature of the Self who is indicated by the word *tvam.*

करणानि हि यद्विषयाभिमुखं प्रगमय्य मतिर्विषयेषु चरेत्।
तदु जागरितं प्रवदन्ति बुधा न तदस्ति ममेत्यवगच्छ दृशेः ॥११०॥

The wise say that the waking state is when the mind engages the senses in their respective sense-objects and moves among the sense-objects. You must understand that the waking state has no relation to Me, the Seeing. (110)

comment

At the time of waking, the mind, under the impulse of experiencing the results of past deeds *(karma),* becomes activated. The mind engages the sense-organs in their respective sense-objects and cognises those objects. The Self or "Seeing" i.e., Awareness, merely reveals the objects of the waking world.

करणानि यदोपरतानि तदा विषयानुभवाहितवासनया।
विषयेण विना विषयप्रतिमं स्फुरणं स्वपनं प्रवदन्ति बुधाः ॥१११॥

The wise say that dream is when the sense-organs have withdrawn [from the sense-objects] and then, in the absence of the sense-object, the mind flashes forth in a form which resembles the sense-object. This is due to mental impressions that are left over from a previous experience of the sense-object. (111)

comment

In dream, the sense-organs are not in contact with their sense-objects, but the mind produces a visual image which resembles something previously experienced in the waking state, even though that object is not present. The mind produces that image under the influence of the mental impressions left over from the experience of an object. Śaṅkara, in his commentary upon the *Bṛhadāraṇyaka* Upaniṣad has said that in dream: "one experiences the mental impressions which resemble objects previously experienced, and which have been revived by desire and the results of past actions." (2.1.18). The Self, the "Seeing", merely illumines the dream world as it illumines the waking world.

करणस्य धियः स्फुरणेन विना विषयाकृतिकेन तु या स्थितता ।
प्रवदन्ति सुषुप्तिममूं हि बुधा विनिवृत्ततृषः श्रुतितत्त्वविदः ॥११२॥

The wise, i.e. those whose thirst [for sense-objects] has ceased and who know the true meaning of the *śruti*, say that dreamless sleep is that state in which the internal-organ [mind] does not flash forth having the form of a sense-object. (112)

comment

A person has three types of experience. In the waking state, there is the empirical subject-object relation: "I see this", "I hear this" etc. This relation is between the external world and the ego "I". The "I" who thinks: "I see this", "I hear this" is the ego, i.e. the mind with the reflection of Awareness. In dream, the sense-organs do not reveal sense-objects as they do in the waking state, but even without the operation of the sense-organs, the mind itself creates a world based upon various experiences derived from the waking state. In dream too there is a subject-object relation between the dreamer and the dream experience. During dreamless sleep the mind does not operate as it did in dream and there is no subject-object relation.

In this verse the teacher reveals that the real meaning of *tvam* is the "Fourth" *(turīya)*.

इति जागरितं स्वपनं च धियः क्रमतोऽक्रमतश्च सुषुप्तिरपि ।

न कदाचिदपि त्रयमस्ति ममेत्यवगच्छ सदास्मि तुरीयमिति ॥११३॥

Thus waking, dream, and dreamless sleep, whether they occur in succession or not, belong to the mind. You must understand: "the three states never belong to Me. I am always the Fourth *(turīya)*." (113)

comment

In whatever order waking, dream and dreamless sleep occur, these states are the three different conditions of the internal-organ *(antaḥkaraṇa)* or "mind". The Self is uniformly present throughout the three states and is called as the "Fourth" *(turīya)* in relation to those three states. The teacher refers to this point in the following verse.

यदु जागरितप्रभृति त्रितयं परिकल्पितमात्मनि मूढधिया ।
अभिधानमिदं तदपेक्ष्य भवेत्परमात्मपदस्य तुरीयमिति ॥११४॥

A person who is deluded superimposes on the Self the three states comprising waking etc. and the supreme Self acquires the name of the "Fourth" *(turīya)* in relation to those states. (114)

comment

The Self is called the "Fourth" or *turīya* in order to distinguish the Self in relation to waking, dream and dreamless sleep. In reality, it is not correct to think that there are four states, waking, dream and dreamless sleep, as well as another state called the "Fourth" or *turīya*. There is actually one real "state", the Self, who is ever present, who neither sleeps, dreams, or awakens. The Self is always the same *(ekarasa)*. If the states of waking, dream and dreamless sleep were as real as the *turīya*, then we could speak of the *turīya* as another state in relation to those three. But they do not all have the same degree of reality. The states of waking, dream and dreamless sleep change and pass, they come and go in the invariable presence of the Self. Therefore there is one real "state" and three *mithyā* states.

The teacher now commences to talk about the apparent nature of duality.

यदपेक्ष्य भवेदभिधानमिदं परमात्मपदस्य तुरीयमिति ।
तदसत्यमसत्यगुणश्च ततः परिनिर्मितवारणचेष्टितवत् ॥११५॥

We have just said that "the supreme Self acquires the name of the "Fourth" *(turīya)* in relation to those states." Those three states are unreal. And the reason is that they are the attributes of what is unreal [i.e. the mind]. It is comparable to the movement of an elephant that someone has made [in puppetry]. (115)

comment

The teacher repeated the sentence from the preceding verse that the word *"turīya"* is only used to distinguish the Self in relation to the states of waking, dream and dreamless sleep. The word "fourth" is only used in relation to these three. But this can be so only if there is a different order of reality between the three states and the "fourth", because if they are of the same order of reality then there must be four states. The teacher makes it clear that there is a different order of reality when he says that "the three states are unreal". By "unreal" *(asatya)* we should understand the technical expression *mithyā*. The word *mithyā* is used to refer to something that cannot be determined to be either completely real, i.e. permanently existing, but neither can that thing be said to be entirely fictitious or imaginary. A thing which is empirically evident, and which cannot be determined to be either permanently real or entirely fictitious *(sadasadbhyām anirvācyam)*, is *mithyā*. The teacher says that the three states are of a different order of reality to the Self. The three states are *mithyā* and the Self is the real substratum. Thus there are not four states, but one real, so called "state", namely the Self, and three *mithyā* states.

In this verse the teacher introduces a lengthy and elaborate discussion about the apparent nature *(mithyātva)* of the world. This topic will continue till verse one hundred and fifty four. In the present verse he presents a reason for saying that the three states are *mithyā*. The reason he gives is that the three states "are the attributes of what is unreal [i.e. the mind]." He had said that: "waking, dream, and dreamless sleep, whether they occur in succession or not, belong to the mind." Therefore, if the mind is *mithyā* the three states must be equally *mithyā* since they are related to three different conditions of the mind. The teacher has presented an inference: the three states are *mithyā*, because they are the attributes of the mind which is *mithyā*, comparable to the movement of an elephant that someone has made. The illustration means that the attribute of what is *mithyā* must be equally *mithyā*, like when someone makes a puppet-elephant, the movements of the puppet are of the same order of reality as the puppet, they do not become the movements of a real elephant.

Now, using the logic provided by the *śruti* itself, the teacher proceeds to substantiate the view that the mind and the three states are *mithyā*.

गगनप्रमुखं पृथिवीचरमं विषयेन्द्रियबुद्धिमनःसहितम् ।
जनिमज्जगदेतदभूतमिति श्रुतयः प्रवदन्त्युपमानशतैः ॥११६॥

The *śruti* texts tell, through hundreds of illustrations, that this world that has originated - comprising everything from space to earth and including sense-objects, sense-organs, intellect and mind - is unreal. (116)

comment

There are many *śruti* texts which speak of the creation of the world. But the *śruti* does not say that the world is real. On the contrary, it tells that the word is *mithyā*.

Where and how does the *śruti* tell that the world is *mithyā?* In the following verse the teacher introduces a discussion about the unreality of the world on the basis of *śruti*.

कफपित्तसमीरणधातुधृतं कुशरीरमिदं सततं हि यथा ।
प्रभवप्रभृति प्रलयान्तमिदं जगदग्निरवीन्दुधृतं हि तथा ॥११७॥

Just as this mortal body is continually maintained by the three humours, phlegm, bile and wind, so is this world, from its origination to its destruction, maintained by fire, the sun and the moon. (117)

comment

The discussion that begins with this verse continues until verse one hundred and twenty seven. The three humours, which are well known in the medical treatises of the Āyurveda, are phlegm *(kapha)*, bile *(pitta)* and air *(vāta)* and their equilibrium sustains the health of the body. The three lights of the world are the fire, the sun and the moon. They sustain this world because in their absence life could not continue.

जगतः स्थितिकारणमित्थमिदं प्रथितं रविवह्निशशित्रितयम् ।
स्मृतिवेदजनेषु भृशं प्रथितं श्रुतिरीरितवत्यनृतं तदिति ॥११८॥

It is well known that this group of three, the sun, fire and the moon, is the reason the world continues in its present way. This is something well known in the traditional teachings *(smṛti)*, in the Veda and to those people who know them. The *śruti* has told that those three are unreal. (118)

How does the *śruti* say that these three, the sun, fire and the moon, are unreal? The teacher answers this in the next verse with reference to the *Chāndogya* Upaniṣad.

यदु रोहितशुक्लसुकृष्णमिदं ज्वलनादिषु रूपमवैति जनः ।
तदु तैजसमाप्यमथान्नमिति ब्रुवती त्रयमेव तु सत्यमिति ॥११९॥

People know that there are red, white and black colours in fire etc. The *śruti* says that those are the colours belonging to [the subtle elements] fire, water and earth respectively. And the *śruti* further says that only the three [elements] are real. (119)

comment

The *Chāndogya* Upaniṣad (6.4.1) says: "The red colour of fire is the colour of [the subtle element] fire, the white colour is the colour of [the subtle element] water and the black colour is the colour of [the subtle element] earth. [In this way] the substantiality of fire disappears. A modification is a name, it depends upon language. The three colours [elements] alone are real." The Upaniṣad continues in the following passages (6.4.2-3) to say that the sun and the moon each have the three colours, red, white and black, and that these are respectively the colours of the three subtle elements: fire, water and food, i.e. earth. The Upaniṣad then says that the substantiality of the sun and moon vanishes as only the three colours are real. The idea is that the three colours represent the three subtle elements. Red is the colour of the subtle element fire *(tejas)*, white is the colour of the subtle element water *(ap)* and black is the colour of the subtle element food *(anna)* or earth. The three subtle elements are the constituents of gross matter as represented by the fire, sun and moon. The gross matter has no inherent substantiality of its own because the gross matter cannot exist separately from its material cause, the three subtle elements. Thus the *śruti* is saying that the subtle constituents are real in relation to gross material forms for the latter have no intrinsic reality of their own. Śaṅkara has also referred to this illustration from the *Chāndogya* Upaniṣad in his commentary upon the *Brahmasūtra* (2.1.14).

The teacher exemplifies this reasoning in the next two verses.

रुचकप्रमुखं कनकादिमयं रुचकाद्यभिधाननिमित्तमपि ।
असदित्यवगम्यत एव यतो व्यभिचारवती रुचकादिमतिः ॥१२०॥

Though the product of gold etc., such as a necklace, is the reason for the use of a name such as "necklace", the necklace is known to be in fact unreal. It is unreal because the idea of "necklace" etc. does not persist. (120)

comment

In this verse the teacher shows that the effect is unreal - correctly speaking we should call it as *mithyā* -in relation to its material cause. In the case of a golden ornament, the ornament seems to be a real entity in its own right for it is the object of an individual word such as "necklace", or "bracelet" etc. But even though there seem to be real entities, each capable of being expressed by its own particular term, and each having a particular function, the ornaments are not real entities. The teacher says the reason why they are unreal is that the idea of the ornament does not persist *(vyabhicarati)*, i.e. the idea of the ornament is not invariable. We say: "this is a golden necklace", "this is a golden bracelet" etc. When we refer to the necklace we exclude the bracelet and vice versa. The ideas of necklace and bracelet are not invariable, whereas the idea of gold persists throughout all cognitions of gold ornaments. Therefore, on the basis of what persists and what does not persist, we say that the gold is more real than the ornaments. The teacher explains this further in the next verse.

न कदाचिदपि व्यभिचारवती कनकादिमतिः पुरुषस्य यतः ।
तत एव हि सत्यतयाभिमतं कनकादि विपर्यय एषु न हि ॥१२१॥

Since a person's idea of the gold etc. never deviates, the gold etc. are therefore accepted as real. There is no reversal in respect of these. (121)

comment

What is invariable is real. The knowledge of gold persists in all ornaments made of gold, whereas the knowledge of the particular ornament does not persist. Therefore gold is more real than the gold ornaments. We do not find the reverse to be true, where the knowledge of gold is variable and knowledge of an ornament is invariable. Therefore the material cause is real in relation to its effects because the knowledge of the material cause persists while the knowledge of the effects does not persist.

Now the teacher relates the illustration of the ornaments and the gold to the *Chāndogya* passage.

रुचकादिसमं ज्वलनादि भवेदनृतत्वगुणेन तु सत्यतया ।
अरुणप्रमुखं ज्वलनप्रभृतिप्रकृतित्रितयं कनकादिसमम् ॥१२२॥

The fire etc. would be equivalent to the necklace etc, since they share the quality of being unreal. The red colour etc., i.e. the triad forming the material cause of the fire and so forth, would be equivalent to the gold etc. on account of being real. (122)

अनयोपमयानृततामवदच्छ्रुतिरग्निदिवाकरचन्द्रमसाम् ।
अमृषात्वमपि श्रुतिरुक्तवती त्रितयस्य तु रक्तपुरःसरिणः ॥१२३॥

Through this type of illustration, the *śruti* has said that fire, the sun and the moon are unreal. The *śruti* has also stated that the three beginning with the red colour are real. (123)

comment

The *Chāndogya* Upaniṣad has supplied a number of illustrations to show that the material cause is real and its effects are *mithyā.* For example: "Just as, my dear, through one lump of clay [being known as the material cause], everything that is made of clay would be known. A modification is a name depending upon language. The clay alone is real." "Just as, my dear, through knowing an ingot of gold everything made of gold would be known. A modification is a name depending upon language. The gold alone is real." (6.1.4-5).

अनृतत्वमिदं ज्वलनप्रभृतेर्यदवादि भवेत्तदुदाहरणम् ।

वितथा विकृतिः सततं सकला न तथा प्रकृतिः श्रुतिनिश्चयतः ॥१२४॥

The unreality of the fire etc. which has been spoken of would be an illustration of the universal proposition *(udāharaṇa).* For what has been ascertained by the *śruti* is that every modification is invariably unreal, but the material cause is not unreal. (124)

comment

The *śruti* has supplied a number of illustrations: the three colours of the fire, sun and moon; clay and all the things made of clay; gold and whatever is made of gold; iron and all the products of iron. These illustrations are used to highlight an underlying reason. In the process of forming an inference, the word *udāharaṇa* stands for the statement of an illustration used along with the *vyāpti* or universal proposition which contains the fundamental reason for the validity of the inference. For instance: "where there is smoke there is fire, as in a kitchen." The example of the kitchen is meant to highlight the universal proposition "where there is smoke there is fire" and the truth of the inference depends upon the validity of that universal proposition. The teacher says that when the *śruti* tells the unreality of the fire and so forth, it is providing an illustration of the universal proposition that the material cause is real and its effects are *mithyā.*

The teacher shows the *mithyātva* of the effects by way of an easily understood example.

प्रदिदर्शयिषुर्वसनस्य यथा वितथत्वमपास्यति तन्तुगुणम् ।
अपकृष्य तु तन्तुसमं त्रितयं ज्वलनप्रमुखस्य तथोक्तवती ॥१२५॥

Just as a person who wants to demonstrate that a garment is unreal removes the strands of threads, in a similar way the *śruti* has stated that the fire and so forth are unreal by separating the three [colours i.e. the three elements] which are analogous to the threads. (125)

comment

If it is asked how the effect is *mithyā*, the teacher presents a common example. A garment is composed of threads which constitute its material cause. If we remove the threads, we are left with a pile of threads, but no garment. The garment is not an independently existing reality, for the existence of the garment depends upon the existence of the threads. When we speak of a "garment" we assume that the garment is a reality in its own right, but actually there is one reality, the threads, and the garment is merely a particular modification of the threads with no existence of its own apart from the existence given to it by language. The modification of the threads gets the name of "garment" and its status as a real entity depends upon language. The garment is transactional, but it is *mithyā*. In this way, the material cause is shown to be real and its various effects are shown to be *mithyā*.

अवनिप्रमुखं वियदन्तमिदं विकृतिस्तु परस्य भवत्यपरम् ।
अनृतं त्वपरं विकृतिस्तु यतोऽवितथं तु परं प्रकृतिस्तु यतः ॥१२६॥

The lower [nature of Brahman], beginning with earth and including space, is the product of the Supreme. The lower is unreal, because it is a product. The Supreme, however, is real, because it is the material cause. (126)

comment

The teacher emphasises that this rule is invariable: the material cause is real and the effects of the material cause are *mithyā*. The "lower nature" *(aparā prakṛti)* is mentioned, for example, in the *Bhagavadgītā* (7.4-5).

He now brings to a close the topic of establishing the *mithyātva* of the world on the basis of the teaching of the *śruti*.

अत एतदसेधि सदुक्ति परं न मृषेति मृषा तु ततोऽन्यदिति ।

इति सिद्धमतो यद्वादि मया जनिमज्जगदेतदभूतमिति ॥१२७॥

Therefore this has been established: the Supreme, referred to by the expression "Being" [i.e. Brahman] is not unreal. Whereas anything other than That is unreal. So what I said before: "this world that has originated is unreal", has been proved. (127)

comment

At the beginning of the topic, in verse one hundred and sixteen, the teacher made the statement that the *śruti* has told that: "this world that has originated - comprising everything from space to earth and including sense-objects, sense-organs, intellect and mind - is unreal."

Having established that the world is *mithyā*, the teacher concludes by referring back to what he had said earlier, in verse one hundred and fifteen, that since the mind is *mithyā*, the three states are also *mithyā*.

मनसोऽप्यनृतत्वमसेध्यमुतः प्रतिपादितहेतुत एव भवेत् ।
चरितं च तदीयमसत्यमतः परिनिर्मितवारणचेष्टितवत् ॥१२८॥

The unreality of the mind has also been established on the basis of the reason that has just been presented. Therefore the activities belonging to the mind must be unreal, like the movement of an elephant that someone has made. (128)

comment

The entire world is *mithyā*, because it is a product, and a product has no independent existence over and above the existence of its material cause. The mind is *mithyā* because the mind too is a product, for it is made of subtle forms of matter. Since the mind is *mithyā*, the activities of the mind, the states of waking, dream, and sleep, would also be *mithyā*. Because the attribute of what is unreal is equally unreal. As an example of this last point, the teacher restates the illustration already given in verse one hundred and fifteen: when someone makes a puppet-elephant, the movements that the unreal elephant makes must also be unreal.

The student raises an objection.

ननु नाभ्यवदच्छ्रुतिरुद्भवनं मनसस्तु सतो न च खप्रमुखात् ।
कथमस्य भवेदनृतत्वगतिर्मनसो भगवन्वद निश्चयतः ॥१२९॥

But the *śruti* has not stated that the mind arises from Brahman, nor has it said that the mind arises from space. How then can you reach the conclusion that the mind is unreal? Reverend sir, tell me decisively! (129)

comment

The student says that even accepting what has been said, namely that the effect of the material cause is unreal, where is it said that the mind is an effect?

The teacher replies.

ननु सप्तम आत्मन उद्भवनं मनसोऽभिदधावसुनापि सह ।
कथमस्य भवेदमृषात्वगतिर्मनसो विकृतित्वगुणस्य वद ॥१३०॥

Why do you say so? In the seventh chapter [the *śruti]* stated that the mind too arises from the Self along with the life-energy. How then can you arrive at the conclusion that the mind is real, when it has the attribute of being a product? You tell me! (130)

comment

The teacher replies that the *śruti* says that the mind has originated. Near the end of the seventh chapter of the *Chāndogya* Upaniṣad it is said that: "...the life-energy is from the Self...the mind is from the Self..." (7.26.1). Therefore the mind is a product, hence it is *mithyā*.

The teacher cites another *śruti.*

असुना करणैर्गगनप्रमुखैः सह मुण्डक उद्भवनं मनसः ।
पुरुषात्परमात्मन उक्तमतो वितथं मन इत्यवधारय भोः ॥१३१॥

In the *Muṇḍaka* it is said that the mind arises from the Puruṣa, the supreme Self, along with the life-energy, the senses and the elements beginning with space. Therefore, O student, you must decisively understand that the mind is unreal! (131)

comment

It is said in the *Muṇḍaka* Upaniṣad: "From the Puruṣa is born the life-energy *(prāṇa),* the mind, all the senses, space, air, fire, water and the earth that supports everything" (2.1.3).

There is a further reason.

मनसोऽन्नमयत्वमवादि यतस्तत एव हि भूतमयत्वगतिः ।
कुशरीरवदेव ततोऽपि भृशं वितथं मन इत्यवधारय भोः ॥१३२॥

Since the mind has been spoken of as a product of food, it has to be understood to be a product of the elements, like the mortal body itself. For this reason also, O student, you must clearly understand that the mind is certainly unreal. (132)

comment

It was said that the mind is *mithyā* because it is a product. Its unreal nature is further specified by showing that the mind is directly a product of the elements. How do we know that the mind is a product of the elements? It is said in the *Chāndogya* Upaniṣad: "The food that is consumed is divided in three ways. The gross constituent of the food becomes faeces. The more subtle constituent becomes flesh and the most subtle part becomes mind" (6.5.1). It is further said: " Dear boy, the mind is a modification of food" (6.6.5).

Now, leaving aside the discussion of *mithyātva* on the basis of the *śruti* and the reasoning implicit in the *śruti,* the teacher proceeds to establish that the world, from the mind onwards, is *mithyā* solely by reasoning. This topic continues until verse one hundred and fifty. He begins with an inference to prove that the effect is unreal.

कुरु पक्षमिमं गगनप्रमुखं जनिमत्सकलं न हि सत्यमिति ।
प्रथमं चरमं च न चास्ति यतो रुचकादिवदित्युपमां च वद ॥१३३॥

You should make this proposition: the entire world that has originated, from space onwards, is not real. The reason is that it does not exist at the beginning and at the end. And you should provide an illustration: like a necklace etc. (133)

He explains the illustration:

कनके रुचकादि न पूर्वमभूच्चरमं च न विद्यत इत्यनृतम् ।
अधुनापि तथैव समस्तमिदं जनिमद्वियदादि भवेदनृतम् ॥१३४॥

The necklace etc. did not exist in the gold before and they do not exist in the gold later. So they are unreal even in the present. In the same way, this entire world that has originated, from space onwards, must be unreal. (134)

comment

The teacher has argued that the world, from the mind onwards, is *mithyā.* His reasoning is that only what persists can be real. This conclusion is shared by all Advaitins. The necklace did not exist before it was fashioned from the gold and it ceases to exist when it is melted down. The gold, however, persists before, during, and after the necklace. So the gold is real and the necklace is *mithyā.* But it may be objected, why cannot we say that the necklace is real at the time that it exists in the gold? The teacher says that the necklace etc. are "unreal even in the present", but how can that be true? The following verses are to demonstrate what the teacher said.

The followers of Nyāya-Vaiśeṣika do not accept that the effect is unreal. On the contrary, they say that the effect is as real as its material cause. The teacher now seeks to demonstrate that the effect is unreal.

कनकादिषु यद्युपजातमभूद्रुचकप्रमुखं पृथगेव ततः ।
अधिकं परिमाणममीषु कुतो न भवेदिति वाच्यमवश्यमिदम् ॥१३५॥

If the necklace and so forth which are present in the gold etc. are indeed separate from the gold etc., then why is there no additional weight in the necklace etc? This is something that surely requires an answer! (135)

comment

The followers of Nyāya-Vaiśeṣika strenuously seek to uphold the commonsense view of the world as real. In order to uphold this position, they must be able to prove that the effect of the material cause is real. For if the effect is not real, then the foundation for their entire doctrine of the reality of the world is undermined. Their teaching regarding the relation of the material cause and its effects is called *asatkāryavāda,* the doctrine of the "origination of the non-existent effect". They say that the effect is an entirely new production in its material cause - they often refer to the material cause as the "inherent cause" *(samavayikāraṇa)* - and the effect exists in the inherent cause through a relation known as "inherence" *(samavāya).* They say, for example, that the piece of gold is the material, or inherent cause, of the gold necklace. When the necklace is made, the necklace is not the same as the gold. The gold continues to exist just as it did before, and it does not transfer its essence to the effect, while a new creation, the necklace, which did not exist before, now appears in the gold. According to Nyāya-Vaiśeṣika, there is not one real thing, the gold, but there are two real things, the gold and the necklace, each having its own separate essence. The gold does not impart its essence to the necklace because the gold continues to exist intact side by side with the necklace. The necklace is a separate entity which exists *in* the gold through the relation called *samavāya*. This doctrine of the Nyāya-Vaiśeṣika is an attempt to avoid the consequence of saying that the effect is a product of the material cause, for then the effect would have no independent existence of its own and therefore the effect can be said to be unreal. Against the Nyāya-Vaiśeṣika position, the teacher makes a criticism which the exponents of Nyāya-Vaiśeṣika have difficulty answering. If the inherent cause, the gold, and the effect, the necklace, are two different realities, why is there no difference between the weight of the gold on its own and the weight of the gold when the necklace exists in the gold? If the necklace is essentially a separate entity, it should make some difference to the measurement of the weight, but no difference in weight can be detected. How can the followers of Nyāya-Vaiśeṣika explain this? They cannot. Therefore their view is an elaborate, but futile, attempt to avoid admitting that the effect is *mithyā*.

कनकप्रभृतेर्व्यतिरिक्तमतो रुचकादि न विद्यत एव कुतः ।
पृथगग्रहणात्कनकप्रभृतेरिति कारणमेव सदन्यदसत् ॥१३६॥

Therefore the necklace etc. do not exist separate from the gold etc. Why? Because they cannot be seen apart from the gold etc. Therefore the material cause is real and what is other [i.e. the effect] is unreal. (136)

comment

The teacher says that there are not two realities, the material cause and its effect. There is only one reality, the material cause. The effect of the material cause has no existence of its own independent of the material cause. If it had a separate existence, then we should be able to apprehend the necklace even if we remove the gold. But upon removing the gold the necklace ceases to exist. Therefore the necklace is transactional but it is *mithyā*. It is a modification possessing a name, but there is no substantive entity that corresponds to the noun "necklace". The only substantive is the material cause.

The student raises an objection.

ननु नाम पृथग्विकृतेः प्रकृतेरथ रूपमथापि च कार्यमतः ।
कथमव्यतिरिक्ततयावगमः प्रकृतेर्विकृतेरिति वाच्यमिदम् ॥१३७॥

Well, the effect has a name, a form and a function distinct from its material cause. How can the effect be understood as non-separate from the material cause? This requires an answer. (137)

comment

The student says that the effect has its own name, its own form and its own function. When the threads are made into a garment, a new name is given to the product, it is no longer called just "threads", so too, the garment has a form and a function different from the threads. Therefore the effect must be an entity in its own right, different from its material cause.

The teacher replies.

इह वीरणतन्तुसुवर्णमृदः कटशाटकहारघटाकृतयः ।
उपलब्धृजनैरुपलब्धिमिता न भिदास्ति ततः प्रकृतेर्विकृतेः ॥१३८॥

Perceptive people here observe that stalks of grass, threads, gold and clay have the form of mats, garments, necklaces and pots. Therefore an effect is not different from its material cause. (138)

comment

The student objected that on account of the difference of name, form and function, we are entitled to infer that the effect is something different from its material cause. The teacher says that we can observe for ourselves that the effect is not different from its material cause.

The teacher further explains.

विकृतिर्यदि नास्ति पृथक्प्रकृतेर्न घटेत भिदाप्यभिधाप्रभृतेः ।
इति धीर्विफला तव येन जनैर्विविदे नयनेन मृदाद्यभिदा ॥१३९॥

Your idea - that if the effect is not distinct from the material cause then even the difference of name and so forth would not be possible - does not amount to anything. Because people know through their perception that [an effect such as a pot etc.] is not different from clay etc. (139)

comment

The student tried to infer that the effect is different from its material cause because the effect has a different name, form and function. If the effect was not different from its material cause, such differences of name, form and function would not be possible. The teacher says that such an inference is worthless because it is disproved by perception, for we can see that an effect has no separate existence apart from its material cause.

The teacher continues.

ननु रूपमथो अपि कार्यमथो अभिधापि नटस्य पृथग्विदिता ।
न पृथक्त्वमुपैति नटः किमिति प्रतिवाच्यमवश्यमिदं कुशलैः ॥१४०॥

Is not an actor known to take on a different form, function and name? Why then does the actor not become different? Let those who are clever [in reasoning i.e., the followers of Nyāya] answer this! (140)

comment

An actor plays a variety of roles, each requiring a different name as well as a different appearance and function. But in spite of these differences, the actor remains the same person. So the differences in name, form and function do not create a real difference. The idea is that even though there can be a difference between the material cause and its effect in terms of name, form and function, these differences do not establish the effect as a reality in its own right apart from its material cause.

In order to show the unreality of the effect, the teacher critiques how the followers of Vaiśeṣika and the followers of Sāṅkhya explain the relation between the effect and its material cause.

असतो न कथञ्चन जन्म भवेत्तदसत्त्वत एव खपुष्पमिव ।
न सतोऽस्ति भवः पुरतोऽपि भवाद्यत आत्मवदेव सदिष्टमिति
॥१४१॥

There is no way that something non-existent can originate, because it does not exist, like a sky-flower does not exist. Nor can something already existent originate, because even prior to its origination it is accepted that it exists, like the Self. (141)

comment

The followers of Nyāyā-Vaiśeṣika uphold the doctrine called *asatkāryavāda*, the doctrine of the "origination of the non-existent effect", which was referred to in the comment to verse one hundred and thirty five. This doctrine says that the effect is an entirely new production in its material cause. For example, due to the operation of the weaver, assisted by the loom and other instruments, threads are woven together and the result is a piece of cloth. According to the Nyāyā-Vaiśeṣika, the threads do not impart their own essence to the cloth. The cloth is an entirely new creation, with its own substance separate from the substance of the threads. The cloth is a new creation which inheres in the threads through a relation that the Nyāyā-Vaiśeṣika called "inherence" *(samavāya)*. This doctrine of "the origination of the non-existent effect" is an attempt to establish that the material cause and the effect are two separate substances. If the effect and the material cause are not separate substances, then the effect must have the same substance as its material cause. Once that is accepted, it can then be shown that the effect is unreal. The Nyāya-Vaiśeṣika seeks to avoid the conclusion that the effect is unreal by proposing this doctrine of "the origination of the non-existent effect".

The Sāṅkhya have a different view from the Nyāyā-Vaiśeṣika. The Sāṅkhya teaching is called *"satkāryavāda"*, the doctrine of "the origination of the existent-effect". Their view is that the effect already exists potentially in its material cause. The cloth potentially exists in the threads and the threads impart their substance to the effect, the cloth. Thus the one substance, the material cause, the threads, transforms into the effect, the cloth. Though the material cause has transformed into the effect, the Sāṅkhya still upholds that the effect is a separate reality. However, their doctrine is closer to the Advaita, for once it is said that the material cause and the effect are the one substance, then it can be argued that the effect is unreal since it has no existence of its own apart from the existence of its material cause.

These teachings may be summed up in this way: the Nyāya-Vaiśeṣika say that the material cause *(dharmin)* and the effect *(dharma)* are different *in essence* from each other. The Sāṅkhya say that the effect *(dharma)* is a changed condition of the material cause *(dharmin)*, the cause and the effect are identical in essence and yet different.

Both the Nyāyā-Vaiśeṣika and the Sāṅkhya believe that the effect is a real entity. The teacher criticises their view in order to show that the effect is *mithyā*. He says that the Nyāyā-Vaiśeṣika view is untenable, for how can something entirely non-existent come into being? If it is a distinct substance, and not the same as the material cause, then where does it come from? It must come out of nothing. How does something come out of nothing? The teacher then says that the Sāṅkhya view too is untenable, because the effect is said to be already potentially existing in the material cause since there is the one substance. So if the effect already exists, how can you speak of its origination?

The teacher now raises a possible objection from a follower of Sāṅkhya in order to clarify what is meant by *satkāryavāda.*

कपिलासुरिपञ्चशिखादिमतं प्रतिगृह्य वदेद्यदि कश्चिदिदम् ।
न कदाचन जन्म वदामि सतः प्रवदामि तु यच्छृणु तत्त्वमपि ॥१४२॥

If someone who accepts the teaching of Kapila, Āsuri, Pañcaśikha etc. would say this: I don't at all say that something existent originates. But you ought listen to what I am saying. (142)

comment

Kapila, Āsuri and Pañcaśikha are mentioned in the *Mokṣadharma* portion of the *Mahābhārata* as early teachers of Sāṅkhya.

The follower of Sāṅkhya explains.

प्रकृतावविशिष्टतया यदभूदधुना तु तदेव विशेषयुतम् ।
निरवद्यमिदं प्रतिभाति मम प्रवदात्र विरोधमवैषि यदि ॥१४३॥

What existed in an attributeless condition in the material cause is now endowed with attributes. This teaching seems faultless to me. If you think there is something incongruous about it, say so. (143)

comment

The Sāṅkhya tradition does not say that the effect, such as a cloth or a pot, is actually existing in its cause before its origination. What it says is that the effect exists potentially, i.e. in an attributeless condition, in its material cause. The cause and the effect are the same in substance, but the effect differs from the cause in that when the cause transforms into the effect, the effect then takes on attributes different from the cause, such as a particular form and function.

The teacher now argues against the Sāṅkhya view in the following two verses.

सदयुज्यत येन गुणेन पुरा प्रकृतौ स इहास्ति न वेति वद ।

यदि विद्यत एव पुरा प्रकृतावधुनापि विशेषयुतत्वमसत् ॥१४४॥

Tell me, that attribute with which the effect became endowed, did it exist in the material cause before [the origination of the effect], or not? If it exists in the material cause even before, [that what you just said] that the effect now becomes endowed with attributes, is false. (144)

comment

The follower of Sāṅkhya said that the effect exists potentially in its material cause in an undifferentiated condition and then acquires attributes which distinguish it as an effect. The teacher asks whether those attributes existed in the material cause before the origination of the effect, or whether they did not exist. In the first alternative, the attributes are already existing in the material cause and so what the follower of Sāṅkhya has just said, namely that: "What existed in an attributeless condition in the material cause is now endowed with attributes" must be untrue.

Taking the alternative, that the attributes do not exist in the material cause before the origination of the effect, the teacher says:

यदि नास्ति पुरा स गुणः प्रकृतावसदुद्भवनं भवतोऽभिमतम् ।
जननेन च सत्त्वमुपात्तवतो जनिमत्त्वत एव विनष्टिरपि ॥१४५॥

If the attribute does not exist in the material cause prior [to the origination of the effect] then you have accepted the origination of the non-existent! And, since there is origination, there would also be the destruction of what has came into being, for the very reason that it has originated. (145)

comment

If the attribute does not exist in the material cause prior to the origination of the effect, then where did the attribute come from? It must have come from nothing! This amounts to accepting the conclusion of the Nyāya-Vaiśeṣika in their doctrine of *asatkāryavāda*, the "origination of the non-existent effect". If the follower of Sāṅkhya says this, then he has contradicted his own teaching that there is no origination of what does not exist. Furthermore, whatever is produced must be impermanent. If something comes into being in time, it cannot be permanent. If the follower of Sāṅkhya accepts the origination of a real effect, that was previously non-existent, he would also have to accept the conclusion that that real thing will also perish. This contradicts his own teaching that there is no destruction of what is real.

भवतोऽभिमतं परिहर्तुमिदं न कथञ्चन शक्यत इत्यमुतः ।
कणभक्षमतेन समत्वमिदं भवतोऽभिमतं शनकैरगमत् ॥१४६॥

There is no way to avoid what you have accepted on the basis of the above reasoning. Your position has ended up equivalent to the doctrine of Kaṇāda! (146)

comment

If the follower of Sāṅkhya accepts what was said in the preceding verse, namely that there is the origination of an attribute which did not previously exist in its material cause, then he cannot deny that he has accepted the origination of something that was non-existent. This amounts to his accepting the *asatkāryavāda* of the Vaiśeṣika tradition founded by Kaṇāda. Thus the follower of Sāṅkhya gradually ends up in agreement with the Vaiśeṣika.

असतो भवनं नशनं च सतः कणभोजिमतं विदितं कविभिः ।
उपपत्तिविरुद्धतया सुभृशं तदभाणि मयापि विरुद्धतया ॥१४७॥

The wise sages understood that Kaṇāda taught the origination of a non-existent effect and the destruction of an existent effect. They have said that this teaching is entirely opposed to reason and I too have said that it is incongruous. (147)

comment

Having shown how the *satkāryavāda* could end up in the *asatkāryavāda,* the teacher says that the doctrine of *asatkāryavāda* is opposed to reason when it says that there is the origination of a real effect which comes to inhere in its "material cause" (or more accurately *samavāyikāraṇa)* through a postulated relation called "inherence" *(samavāya).* According to this doctrine, the effect is real; the effect is different in essence from the material cause; and the effect comes to exist in the cause, as for example cloth comes to inhere in the threads, through the relation called *samavāya.* Since the material cause and the effect are different in essence, this teaching amounts to saying that a real effect has come into being out of nothing. In the effort to establish that the effect is real in its own right, the Vaiśeṣika has ended up in this untenable position.

प्रतिषिद्धमिदं कणभोजिमतं हरिणापि समस्तगुरोर्गुरुणा ।
वचनेन तु नासत इत्यमुना ब्रुवता च पृथातनयाय हितम् ॥१४८॥

Hari, the teacher of all teachers, has also denied this doctrine of Kaṇāda with the statement "the non-existent has no real being", and he said this to benefit Arjuna. (148)

comment

In the *Bhagavadgītā,* Śrī Kṛṣṇa, the incarnation of Lord Viṣṇu, taught Arjuna, the son of Pṛthā, i.e. Kuntī, that the non-existent does not come into being and the existent does not cease to be. He said: "The non-existent has no real being and the existent does not cease to be. Those who perceive the truth have seen the true nature of them both." (2.16). He said this to teach the real nature of things to Arjuna.

To complete the refutation of the origination of either an existent effect or a non-existent effect, the teacher refers, in passing, to the Jaina doctrine.

असतश्च सतश्च न जन्म भवेदिति पूर्वमवाद्युपपत्तियुतम् ।
सदसञ्च न जायत एव कुतो न हि वस्तु तथाविधमस्ति यतः ॥१४९॥

It was previously stated, with reasoning, that there can be no birth of a non-existent effect nor of an existent effect. An effect which is both existent and non-existent most certainly does not originate. Why? Because there is no such thing! (149)

comment

The Jains say that the Vedānta position is wrong, they say that it is not true that the material cause, the substantive *(dharmi)* is alone real and the attributes*(dharma)* are all *mithyā.* However they also disagree with those, such as the Buddhists, who say that there is no substantive and all that exists are a collection of attributes. The Jains try to reconcile both positions in a "common sense" view that in everything there is both reality and unreality. In any object, there is both permanence and as well as change. The clay is a real substantive but it has various changing attributes, such as the pot form etc. In response to this attempt to uphold common sense appearance, the Vedāntin says that the Jain cannot simultaneously hold contradictory propositions about the same entity. The Jain cannot say that the effect is simultaneously real and unreal.

सदसत्त्वमतीत्य मनःप्रभृतेर्न कथञ्चन वृत्तिरिहास्ति यतः ।
तत एव मनःप्रमुखस्य भवो न भवेदिति सर्वसुवेद्यमिति ॥१५०॥

Since [the world] from the mind onwards has no way of existing once we have crossed over either the existence or the non-existence [of the effect in relation to its material cause], therefore, there can be no origination of [the world] starting with the mind. Everyone should know this. (150)

comment

Once we give up the explanation of *satkāryavāda*, that the effect is already potentially existing in its material cause, and *asatkāryavāda*, that the effect is not potentially existing in its material cause, there is no way to explain how the effect can originate from its material cause. While the effect like a pot or a cloth etc. is a transactional *(vyāvahārika)* entity, it is not a reality in its own right because it is not a substantive existing alongside the material cause. When we look at the effect from a transactional viewpoint *(vyāvahārikadṛṣti)* we must conclude that the effect is *mithyā* and that its origin is inexplicable *(anirvācya)* for it cannot be explained by resorting to either the *satkāryavāda*, or the *asatkāryavāda*, and there is no other possible explanation. When we look at the effect from the absolute standpoint *(pāramārthikadṛṣṭi)* then there is no effect because the so called effect has no existence apart from the material cause. The word origination implies that something has really come into being, but when the effect is not a substantive how could it come into being? Therefore, the *mithyā* effect has a *mithyā* origination, but not a real origination. This is the "Ajātivāda" taught by Gauḍapāda.

यदि नाम कथञ्चिदमुष्य भवः सदसत्त्वमपेक्ष्य भविष्यति वः ।
अमृषात्वममुष्य तथापि न तु श्रुतिरस्य मृषात्वमुवाच यतः ॥१५१॥

Even if you think that the world, beginning with the mind, does somehow originate according to either the prior existence or the non-existence [of the effect], even then it is not real. For the *śruti* has declared that it is unreal. (151)

comment

The teacher says that even if we were to accept for the sake of argument that the effect does somehow come into being according to either the *satkāryavāda* or *asatkāryavāda*, even then we cannot say that what has originated is real. For the *śruti* has explicitly declared the unreality of the effects in such statements as in the *Chāndogya:* "Just as, my dear, through one lump of clay [being known as the material cause], everything that is made of clay would be known. A modification is a name depending upon language. The clay alone is real." (6.1.4).

The teacher now concludes this discussion.

मनसोऽनृततैवमवादि यतस्तत एव हि तस्य मृषा चरितम् ।
यत एव मृषा मनसश्चरितं तत एव पुरोदितसिद्धिरभूत् ॥१५२॥

Since in this way the mind has been said to be unreal, it follows that the activities of the mind are unreal. And since the activities of the mind are unreal, what I said before has been proved. (152)

comment

The *śruti* has told that all the modifications are *mithyā* and it has been shown by reasoning that other teachings about a real origination are flawed. So what was first said in verse one hundred and fifteen is now established. In the following verse, the teacher restates what he had said in verse one hundred and fifteen.

यदपेक्ष्य तु नाम भवेत्त्रितयं परमात्मपदस्य तुरीयमिति ।
तदसत्यमसत्यगुणस्तु यतः परिनिर्मितसर्पविसर्पणवत् ॥१५३॥

The supreme Self acquires the name of the "Fourth" *(turīya)* in relation to the three states. Those states are unreal, because they are the attributes of what is unreal [i.e. the mind]. It is like the gliding motion of a snake that someone has made. (153)

comment

The mind is *mithyā* because the mind is an effect, it is made of the subtle constituents of matter *(nāmarūpa)* and Brahman is the material cause of the *nāmarūpa*. Also, the mind is *mithyā* because we cannot ascertain how an effect can really originate according to either *satkāryavāda* or *asatkāryavāda*. Since the mind is *mithyā*, the functions of the mind are also *mithyā*. The functions of the mind are the various cognitive activities of the mind. The waking state, the dream state and the state of dreamless sleep are connected to the functioning of the mind. Therefore the three states are *mithyā* as they are the functions of the mind which is *mithyā*. For example, if the snake appearing on the rope is *mithyā*, then the movement of that snake is also *mithyā*, for if something is unreal then its attributes must be equally unreal. The reality is called the "fourth" only in relation to the other three states. Since the three states are unreal, the word "fourth" becomes just a mere designation, which was useful as a means to reveal the reality. The fact is that there is one absolute "state", which is unchanging and therefore real. It is called the Self (Ātman), or Brahman. Everything else is *mithyā*.

निखिलस्य मनःप्रमुखस्य यतो वितथत्वमवादि पुरा तु मया ।
श्रुतियुक्तिबलेन ततोऽद्वयकं परमक्षरमेव सदन्यदसत् ॥१५४॥

Since I have just stated, on the strength of *śruti* and reasoning, that this entire world beginning with the mind is unreal, therefore, the supreme Imperishable, free from duality, is alone real. Anything other is unreal. (154)

comment

The Self is free from duality because duality is shown to be *mithyā* and the *mithyā* duality does not constitute a reality in its own right.

The teacher now refers to the *śruti* to show that his *siddhānta* is in accord with what the *śruti* teaches.

यदपूर्वमबाह्यमनन्तरकं न च किञ्चन तस्य भवत्यपरम् ।
इति वेदवचोऽनुशशास यतो वितथं परतोऽन्यदतः प्रगतम् ॥१५५॥

प्रतिषिध्य यतो बहिरन्तरपि स्वविलक्षणमात्मन उक्तवती ।
अवबोधघनत्वमतोऽन्यदसल्लवणैकरसत्वनिदर्शनतः ॥१५६॥

Since the statement of the Veda has taught that Brahman does not have anything that precedes [i.e. some cause], does not have anything that is exterior or interior, and does not have anything subsequent [i.e. some effect], it is thereby clearly understood that anything other than the supreme Imperishable is unreal. (155)

The *śruti,* using the illustration of the homogeneity of the taste of salt, negated anything other, whether internal or external, and stated that the Self is homogeneous Awareness, therefore anything other is unreal. (156)

comment

In the *Bṛhadāraṇyaka* Upaniṣad there is the passage: "Brahman is without prior or posterior, without interior or exterior" (2.5.19). The idea is that Brahman is not the effect of anything, nor is Brahman the cause of anything, nor is there anything inside or outside Brahman. Therefore anything which appears as something "other" than Brahman is unreal. Verse one hundred and fifty six refers to the following *Bṛhadāraṇyaka* passage: "As a lump of salt is without interior or exterior, entire, and has just an indivisible taste, even so, my dear, this Self is without interior or exterior, entire, and is solely a mass of Intelligence" (4.5.13). Here, the *śruti* negates that there is anything interior or exterior to Brahman and then points out the nature of Brahman as a "mass of Intelligence". Therefore Brahman is non-dual because anything "other" i.e., the world of name-and-form, is *mithyā.*

लवणैकरसत्वसमं भणितं स्वविलक्षणवस्तुनिषेधनतः ।
अवबोधघनं परमात्मपदं त्वमवेहि तदस्मि सदाहमिति ॥१५७॥

Following the negation of anything other, the supreme Self was spoken of as a mass of Awareness, analogous to the homogeneity of the taste of salt. You must have the understanding: "I am always That!" (157)

To help the student understand, in the following two verses the teacher again clarifies the meaning of *"tat"* and *"tvam"*. In this verse he indicates the meaning of *"tat"*.

अणु नो न च तद्विपरीतगुणं न च ह्रस्वमतो न च दीर्घमपि ।
प्रतिषिद्धसमस्तविशेषणकं परमक्षरमात्मतयाश्रय भोः ॥१५८॥

It is not minute, nor does It have the opposite attribute. It is not short, nor is It long. O student, you must come to accept the supreme Imperishable, from which all distinguishing characteristics have been negated, as your Self! (158)

comment

This verse is similar to verse one hundred and eight and verse one hundred and nine.

He indicates the meaning of *"tvam"*.

असुबुद्धिशरीरगुणान् षडिमानविवेकिजनैर्दृशिधर्मतया ।
प्रतिपन्नतमान् प्रविहाय शनैर्दृशिमात्रमवेहि सदाहमिति ॥१५९॥

Giving up the six attributes that pertain to the vital-breath, to the mind and to the physical body - attributes which indiscriminating people have thoroughly accepted to be the properties of the Seeing - you must gradually come to the understanding: "I am always pure Seeing." (159)

comment

The six qualities are hunger, thirst, sorrow, delusion, infirmity and death. Hunger and thirst are qualities of the vital-breath *(prāṇa).* Sorrow and delusion are qualities of the mind and infirmity and death are qualities pertaining to the physical body. People implicitly accept these as attributes of the Self. According to the Upaniṣads, neither the *prāṇā*, nor the mind, nor the physical body, nor their attributes, are the essential Self who is Brahman.

The Advaita tradition is founded upon the understanding of the Upaniṣads as revelation. If the Upaniṣads did not reveal that there is an absolute Reality, people would not by themselves orient their outlook in this way. On the basis of perception and inference, people naturally believe that they are real individual selves, and think of themselves as identical with their physical body. Or, if people begin to analyse this so-called "self", they may determine that there is no enduring entity apart from the processes of the body-sense-mind complex itself. This is the Buddhist position. Thus without the Upaniṣads, people would not normally so much as suspect that there is a fundamental Reality, which is non-dual.

The Upaniṣads reveal that there is such a Reality. Furthermore they reveal that one's own essential nature is That *(ayam ātmā brahma; tasmād etasmād ātmanaḥ; tat tvam asi;* etc.). They further reveal that this Reality *(vastu)* is Being Itself *(sat),* which is identical to "Seeing" or pure Awareness *(cit),* and It is without limit *(ananta)* (as for instance: *satyaṁ jñānam anantaṁ brahma; prajñānaṁ brahma; sarvānubhūḥ; nānyad ato'sti draṣṭṛ; na hi draṣṭur dṛṣṭer viparilopo vidyate, avināśitvāt; eko draṣṭādvaito bhavati; yan manasā na manute yenāhur mano matam;* etc.). Thus the Upaniṣads reveal that there is an absolute Reality and they reveal that you are That. Padmapāda, near the beginning of his *Pañcapādikā,* has said: "The fundamental purport of the *śāstra* [referring to the *Brahmasūtra]* is that the Vedānta culminates in showing that the ultimate nature of the Self - who is under the apprehension of being a suffering, mortal, entity - is solely and simply immutable Awareness, which is complete happiness and is identical to Being."

In order to directly understand this teaching, which is a teaching of "you *are* That" and not "you will *become* That", the Upaniṣads have a twofold method, they negate and reveal. They negate, by discrimination, all the objective and transient features of the person that are mistakenly attributed to the Self. Their revelation consists in that they point out that Brahman exists and they further reveal that the essential Self of the person is Brahman. The result of the twofold method is the awakening to the knowledge that the Self is actually the One Awareful Seeing, ever pure, conscious and free *(nityaśuddhabuddhamuktasvabhāva).*

The teacher now tells about liberation while living *(jīvanmukti).*

अहिनिर्ल्वयनीमहिरात्मतया जगृहे परिमोक्षणतस्तु पुरा ।
परिमुच्य तु तामुरगः स्वबिले न पुनः समवेक्षत आत्मतया ॥१६०॥

अविवेकत आत्मतया विदितं कुशरीरमिदं भवताप्यहिवत् ।
अहिवत्त्यज देहमिमं त्वमपि प्रतिपद्य चिदात्मकमात्मतया ॥१६१॥

Prior to shedding its skin, a snake accepts the slough as its Self. But once the snake has shed the slough in its hole, it no longer looks upon the slough as its Self. (160)

Like the snake, you also have thought that this mortal body is the Self, owing to a lack of discrimination. Once you have understood yourself to be Awareness, you too must give up this body, as the snake gave up its slough. (161)

comment

In the *Bṛhadāraṇyaka* Upaniṣad, Yājñavalkya teaches Janaka about the person who is liberated and living: "Just as the lifeless slough of a snake would lie cast off on an ant-hill, just so does this body lie. Then this liberated person is bodiless, immortal, the Self, Brahman, the light of Awareness" (4.4.7). Just like the snake casts off its slough, the liberated person casts off the notion of being the body. The snake continues to live after shedding its old skin, so too the liberated person continues to live in the body after shedding the notion of being the body. The liberated person abandons the body solely through knowing that one's essential nature is not the complex of *nāma-rūpa* that is the body. The liberated person continues to live *(jīvanmukta)*, experiencing the various results of karma *(prārabdhakarma)*, the variety of pleasures and pains that the body must undergo. But the liberated person knows that all this pertains merely to the body, not to the Self. The liberated person is no longer under the sway of the demands of the body or the desires of the mind, but lives free from narrow, ego-centred concerns.

The teacher now conveys to the student the understanding of the *jīvanmukta.* Here, he points out that knowledge and ignorance both pertain to the mind, not to the Self.

रजनीदिवसौ न रवेर्भवतः प्रभया सततं युत एष यतः ।
अविवेकविवेकगुणावपि तौ भवतो न रवेरिव नित्यदृशेः ॥१६२॥

The sun has neither day nor night, because the sun is always luminous. So too, the attribute of discrimination and the lack of discrimination do not belong to You, the constant Seeing, who is analogous to the sun. (162)

comment

Neither the knowledge of one's real nature, nor the ignorance of one's nature, belong to the Self, the constant, self-luminous, Seeing. Knowledge and ignorance pertain to the mind, not to the Self. The ego is a function of the mind. The teacher has already taught that the ego is a function of the mind in verses fourteen and fifteen. Both ignorance and knowledge are conditions of the mind, so there is either an ignorant ego, who is a *saṁsārī,* or there is an enlightened "ego" who is a *jīvanmukta.* These conditions do not pertain to the Self.

परिशुद्धविबुद्धविमुक्तदृशेरविवेकविवेकविवर्जनतः ।
मम बन्धविमोक्षगुणौ भवतो न कदाचिदपीत्यवगच्छ भृशम् ॥१६३॥

You must understand this well: because of being free from either discrimination or the absence of discrimination, the attributes of bondage or liberation never belong to Me, the Seeing that is completely pure, awareful and free. (163)

comment

Since discrimination and the lack of discrimination belong to the mind and not to the Self, liberation and bondage pertain to the mind but not to the Self, Brahman, the pure Seeing *(dṛśi)*, which is by nature ever pure, awareful and free *(nityaśuddhabuddhamukta)*.

न मम ग्रहणोज्झनमस्ति मया न परेण दृशेरिति निश्चिनु भोः।
न हि कस्यचिदात्मनि कर्म भवेन्न च कश्चिदिहास्ति मदन्य इति ॥१६४॥

O student, you must ascertain like this: "I, the Seeing, am neither attained nor abandoned, either by myself or by someone else." For no one can have their own Self as their object. And there is no one here other than Me. (164)

comment

Even if the Self is beyond bondage and liberation, it could be thought that the seeker must attain the Self, perhaps through the cultivation of some type of trance experience. The teacher rejects this idea as well. The idea of attainment is predicated upon the wrong understanding that there is a real ego subject who attains an object that is not already possessed, analogous to how the ego attains some object in the world. But when the thing to be attained is already in one's possession, then the idea of attaining becomes meaningless. What is called "Brahman" is the self-luminous Awareness, or Experience *per se*, which cannot be "attained" because it is always identical to one's Self. Brahman has to be clearly recognised in terms of knowing and being. The teacher says Brahman can neither be attained or relinquished, either by oneself or by another. Brahman cannot be attained by oneself because "no one can have their own Self as their object", i.e. the Self cannot be both the subject and the object. The whole idea of attaining is metaphorical from the standpoint of Brahman as the ever-present Self.

The teacher also says that Brahman is not attained by someone else, because there is no other Self. He refers to this in the next verse.

अहमस्मि चरस्थिरदेहधियां चरितस्य सदेक्षक एक इति ।
न भवेदत एव मदन्य इति त्वमवेहि सुमेध इदं सुदृढम् ॥१६५॥

O intelligent man, you must know this with certainty: "I am always the single Seer of the activity belonging to the minds of whatever is moving or immobile." That is why there can be no other than Me. (165)

comment

The Self or Brahman is the pure Awareness-Being, the self-luminous I that cannot become an object, it is That by which everything is illumined. While the self-reflexive cognition called the "individual self" differs in each body, the non-reflexive, self-luminous Seer or "witness", is one in all beings. The I is one because all difference is based upon some distinction and all distinction pertains to the *upādhi* of the body-sense-mind complex, not to That which reveals the *upādhi.*

The teacher gives an example.

गगने विमले जलदादिमले सति वासति वा न भिदास्ति यथा ।
त्वयि सर्वगते परिशुद्धदृशौ न भिदास्ति तथा द्वयभेदकृता ॥१६६॥

Just as there is no difference in the pure sky whether the impurities of clouds etc. are present or not, so too, in You, the all-pervasive pure Seeing, there is no difference caused by duality. (166)

comment

There is no division in space due to the presence of clouds, columns of smoke etc. Nor is there any change in space due to the absence of these things. The teacher says that the Self is not touched by the presence or absence of the duality caused by *nāmarūpa*, such as the body-sense-mind complex.

But then do you admit that there is duality? The teacher says:

अनृतं द्वयमित्यवदाम पुरा व्यवहारमपेक्ष्य तु गीतमिदम् ।
अनृतेन न सत्यमुपैति युजां न मरीचिजलेन नदी ह्रदिनी ॥१६७॥

We have said before that duality is unreal. The duality just spoken of is with reference to ordinary dealings. The real does not enter into relation with the unreal. A river does not become deep through connection to the water of a mirage. (167)

comment

The relation between what is real and what is *mithyā* cannot be a real relation. The *satyam* Brahman plus the *mithyā nāmarūpa jagat* do not add up to duality because there are not two real things, there is only one real.

The teacher now concludes the discussion. He again points out to the student the meaning of the word I.

बहुनाभिहितेन किमु क्रियते शृणु संग्रहमत्र वदामि तव ।
त्वयि जागरितप्रभृति त्रितयं परिकल्पितमित्यसदेव सदा ॥१६८॥

परिकल्पितमित्यसदित्युदितं मन इत्यभिशब्दितमागमतः ।
उपपत्तिभिरेव च सिद्धमतो भवतोऽन्यदशेषमभूतमिति ॥१६९॥

What is gained by more being said? Listen, I will now state it briefly for you. The three states, comprising the waking state and so forth, are superimposed in You. So they are always unreal. (168)

On the basis of the *śāstra*, what is called as "mind" is found to be superimposed and unreal. And this has been proved by reasoning as well. Therefore, whatever is other than You is unreal. (169)

comment

The teacher briefly refers to what he has told before. The three states of experience, waking, dream and dreamless sleep, were discussed in verses one hundred and ten to one hundred and fifteen. This analysis of the three states was for the purpose of clarifying the real meaning of I. The teacher said in verse one hundred and thirteen that the three states are related to the functioning of the mind and he then went on to elaborately argue, up to verse one hundred and fifty four, that the mind is *mithyā* and so the three states must equally be *mithyā*.

And he points out the meaning of the word Brahman and the identity of the Self and Brahman.

यद्बाह्यमनन्तरमेकरसं यदकार्यमकारणमद्वयकम् ।
यदशेषविशेषविहीनतरं दृशिरूपमनन्तमृतं तदसि ॥१७०॥

What is without exterior, without interior, and is partless, what is without an effect, without a cause and is free from duality, what is completely devoid of all distinguishing characteristics: you are That, the pure Seeing, limitless and real. (170)

comment

The *Bṛhadāraṇyaka* Upaniṣad teaches that Brahman is: "without prior or posterior, without interior or exterior" (2.5.19). The idea is that Brahman is not the effect of anything, nor is Brahman the cause of anything, nor is there anything inside or outside Brahman. This was mentioned in verse one hundred and fifty five. Brahman is partless *(ekarasa)* Awareness, for there is the *Bṛhadāraṇyaka* passage: "As a lump of salt is without interior or exterior, entire, and has just an indivisible *(ekarasa)* taste, even so, my dear, this Self is without interior or exterior, entire, and is solely a mass of Intelligence" (4.5.13). This was mentioned in verse one hundred and fifty six. The phrase "limitless and real" was mentioned earlier, in verse six. It refers to the passage in the *Taittirīya* Upaniṣad: "Brahman is real, Awareness, limitless" (2.1.1). When the meaning of I is clarified, so that there is no longer any doubt or confusion that I essentially means pure Awareness, then there is no obstacle to understanding that the real meaning of I is identical to what is revealed to be the meaning of "That".

The instruction is now concluded.

इयदेव मयोपनिषत्सु पदं परमं विदितं न ततोऽस्त्यधिकम् ।
इति पिप्पलभक्ष इवाभ्यवदद्ध्यवशिष्टमतिं विनिवारयितुम् ॥१७१॥

To remove the idea that something remained to be taught, the teacher spoke as Pippalāda had spoken: "Just so much do I know the supreme Being in the Upaniṣads. There is nothing in addition to this." (171)

comment

At the conclusion of the *Praśna* Upaniṣad, the sage Pippalāda told his students: "I know the supreme Brahman thus far. There is nothing beyond this" (6.7). Śaṅkara comments that Pippalāda said this: "to remove the doubt of the students that something remains which they have not learnt, and to engender the conviction that they had accomplished their purpose."

The student addresses the teacher.

इतरोऽपि गुरुं प्रणिपत्य जगौ भगवन्निति तारितवानसि माम् ।
अवबोधतरेण समुद्रमिमं मृतिजन्मजलं सुखदुःखझषम् ॥१७२॥

The other one then prostrated to the teacher and spoke: O holy sir, on the raft of knowledge you have brought me across this ocean whose waters are birth and death and where the fish are pleasures and pains! (172)

comment

This verse refers to what the student had said to the teacher at the beginning, in verse four. The present verse is reminiscent of the concluding passage from the *Praśna* Upaniṣad: "While honouring him they said: 'you indeed are our father, you have brought us to the further shore beyond ignorance'." (6.8).

अधुनास्मि सुनिर्वृत आत्मरतिः कृतकृत्य उपेक्षक एकमनाः ।
प्रहसन्विषयान्मृगतोयसमान्विचरामि महीं भवता सहितः ॥१७३॥

Now I am fully contented, I find my delight in the Self, I have fulfilled my purpose. I am detached, my mind is composed. Laughing at sense objects, which resemble the waters of a mirage, I will roam the earth along with you! (173)

तव दास्यमहं भृशमामरणात्प्रतिपद्य शरीरधृतिं भगवन् ।
करवाणि मया शकनीयमिदं तव कर्तुमतोऽन्यदशक्यमिति ॥१७४॥

Holy sir, accepting whatever comes to maintain the body, I shall serve you devotedly till death. This I can do for you. I cannot do other than this! (174)

comment

The student's statement is reminiscent of what Janaka had said in the *Bṛhadāraṇyaka* Upaniṣad, at the conclusion of his dialogue with

Yājñavalkya: "I will give you, holy sir, the country of Videha, along with me also at your service!" (4.4.23).

The dialogue between the teacher and the student is over. Toṭaka now concludes the text.

गुरुशिष्यकथाश्रवणेन मया श्रुतिवच्छ्रुतिसारसमुद्धरणम् ।
कृतमित्थमवैति य एतदसौ न पतत्युदधौ मृतिजन्मजले ॥१७५॥

I composed the *Śrutisārasamuddharaṇa* ("Extracting the Essence of the Śruti") in this way by listening to the discussions that took place between the teacher and students, discussions that were like *śruti* itself. A person who understands this treatise will not fall into that ocean whose waters are birth and death. (175)

Toṭaka emphasises the importance of devotion to the teacher by making it the qualification for studying this work.

भगवद्भिरिदं गुरुभक्तियुतैः पठितव्यमपाठ्यमतोऽन्यजनैः ।
गुरुभक्तिमतः प्रतिभाति यतो गुरुणोक्तमतोऽन्यभजन्न पठेत् ॥१७६॥

Those holy ones, who have devotion to the guru, are entitled to study this work. People not of this type should not study it. For what the guru has said becomes directly evident when a person has devotion to the guru, that is why someone who is devoted to other things should not study this. (176)

निगमोऽपि च यस्य इतिप्रभृतिर्गुरुभक्तिमतः कथितं गुरुणा ।
प्रतिभाति महात्मन इत्यवदत्पठितव्यमतो गुरुभक्तियुतैः ॥१७७॥

The Veda, in the passage: "the person who has [supreme devotion to the Deity and as much devotion to the guru]" has said that what the teacher speaks becomes clear to that great person who has devotion to the guru. That is why those who have devotion to the guru are entitled to study this. (177)

comment

The passage referred to comes from the last verse of the *Śvetāśvatara* Upaniṣad: "The things which have been told become clear to that great person who has supreme devotion to the Deity and has as much devotion to the spiritual teacher as to the Deity" (6.23).

In the final two verses Toṭaka praises his own guru and the Lord.

येषां धीसूर्यदीप्त्या प्रतिहतमगमन्नाशमेकान्ततो मे
ध्वान्तं स्वान्तस्य हेतुर्जननमरणसन्तानदोलाधिरूढेः ।
येषां पादौ प्रपन्नाः श्रुतिशमविनयैर्भूषिताः शिष्यसङ्घाः
सद्यो मुक्ताः स्थितास्तान्यतिपरमहितान्यावदायुर्नमामि ॥१७८॥

The darkness [i.e. ignorance] of my mind, which was the cause of my being caught up in the swing of the ceaseless movement of birth and death, was entirely destroyed when it was opposed by the light of the sun in the form of the intelligence of my teacher. Groups of students, endowed with knowledge of the *śruti*, tranquillity and humility, quickly became liberated once they came to his feet. As long as I live I salute that teacher, the very greatest among ascetics. (178)

comment

This verse closely resembles, in both the use of language as well as meaning, the verse at the end of the *Māṇḍūkya bhāṣya*, where Śaṅkara salutes his own teacher.

भूः पादौ यस्य खं चोदरमसुरनिलश्चन्द्रसूर्यौ च नेत्रे
कर्णावाशाः शिरो द्यौर्मुखमपि दहनो यस्य वास्तव्यमब्धिः ।
अन्तःस्थं यस्य विश्वं सुरनरखगगोभोगिगन्धर्वदैत्यैः,
चित्रं रंरम्यते तं त्रिभुवनवपुषं विष्णुमीशं नमामि ॥१७९॥

I bow down to Lord Viṣṇu, whose body comprises the three worlds. His feet are the earth, the cavity of His belly is space, His vital-breath is the wind and His eyes are the sun and the moon. His ears are the directions, His head is the heaven, His face is the fire and His bladder is the ocean. Within Him this universe delights with its variety of gods, human beings, birds, cows, snakes, celestial beings and demons. To that Viṣṇu I offer my salutations. (179)

comment

The final verse refers to Viṣṇu as *virāṭ,* i.e. Viṣṇu whose form is the physical universe itself. This verse is based upon the *Puruṣa Sūkta* which speaks of Viṣṇu as the *virāḍrūpam,* as the material cause of the universe. This verse completes the *Śrutisārasamuddharaṇam* of Śrī Toṭakācārya.

This small commentary, which is meant as a help to understand the teaching in the absence of hearing the text directly from the mouth of a true teacher, is also complete.

संश्रुत्योपनिषद्वाचः संप्रसुता मुखाद् यस्य ।
मुमुक्षुबोधसाहाय्यं व्याखानमेतदर्पितम् ॥१॥
तं नमामि दयानन्दं वन्दे च तं महाविष्णुम् ।
यस्य रूपमिदं विश्वं यत्तत्त्वं च चिदात्मकम् ॥२॥

After attentively listening to the words of the Upaniṣads that poured forth from the mouth of that [teacher], I have offered this commentary to assist the understanding of seekers. I salute that [teacher] Dayānanda. And I pay homage to that great Viṣṇu, whose form is this universe and whose essence is Awareness.

APPENDIX

APPENDIX

Variant readings between the Vani Vilas Edition and the Anandashrama Edition
(the preferred reading in this text is indicated by *)

	Sri Vani Vilas	Anandashram
v.3	yatidharmato (misprint)	yatidharmarato *
v.8	tadā janadhīcaritam	sadā* janacittaratam*
v.22	atha*	atho
v.26	kaṇādamate*	kaṇādakṛte
v.28	na parityajatā	tvaparityajatā*
v.30	nityam ataḥ*	ity amutaḥ
v.35	etam aham	etad aham*
v.39	abhyavadat*	apy avadat
v.49	yata evam ato*	tata eva matam
v.53	svakam eṣa*	svakam eva

v.58	yadā/tadā*	yathā/tathā
v.61	yadā/tadā*	yathā/tathā
v.75	...guṇoktir*	guṇoktikatā
v.76	na ca* (Kailās Āśram Ed.=na ca)	iha
v.94	tat tvam iti*	tattvamatim
v.96	na na hāsyati (we have followed the Kailās Āśram Ed., na jahāsyati)*	na jihāsati...na
v.100	na nityam iti pragatam*	na nityamatipragatam
v.102	aviyuktatayā*	avimuktatayā
v.109	adhīkam* virajaskam*	abuddhim arajaskam
v.112	amum	amūm*
v.113	suṣuptir* sadā*	suṣuptam tadā
v.118	prathitam*	yad iti
v.120	api*	iti
v.138	upalabdhim itā*	upalabdham ato
v.142	āsuri*	āsura
v.143	avaśiṣṭatayā	aviśiṣṭatayā*
v.150	sarvasuvedam	sarvasuvedyam*

v.158	viparītaguṇam*	viparītaguṇo
v.162	yuta eṣa yataḥ* tau*	yata eṣa yutaḥ te
v.166	jaladādimale*	jaladādimateḥ
v.168	tataḥ	tava*
v.176	anyabhajan*	anyarato
v.178	sadyo muktāḥ* yativaramahitān	sadyo muktau yatiparamahitān*
v.179	khaṁ codaram* vāsteyam	nābhir viyat vāstavyam*